QUESTIONS PRESENTED

Whether this court should reverse the decision of the Sixth Circuit, and direct the District Court:

1. To apply the doctrine of Equitable Tolling and reinstate petitioner's original FDCPA claim;

2. To reinstate petitioners additional (or new) FDCPA claim that arose during the district court proceedings;

3. To reinstate Petitioner's Title 42 §§ 1983 and 1985 claims until the court decides whether state court jurisdiction over the petitioners comports with the 14th amendment to the U.S. Constitution;

4. To direct the district court to rule on petitioner's several motions left unresolved at the time of dismissal, which were not reviewed by the Sixth Circuit.

5. To stay the state court proceedings under 28 U.S.C. § 1651 until the respondents have complied with all district court orders and the matter of state court jurisdiction is resolved.

TABLE OF CONTENTS

OPINIONS BELOW..1
INTRODUCTION...6
ARGUMENT..8

    1. The FDCPA Claim of April 10, 2017.......8

    2. The Original FDCPA Claim..................10

    3. Fraudulent Concealment.....................12

    4. Challenge of State Court Jurisdiction....15

    5. Revised Amended Complaint...............18

    6. Urgent Motion for a Stay.....................19

    7. Judicial Notice of Case No. 00227.........19

REASONS TO GRANT THE WRIT 27

    I. A WRIT OF MANDAMUS IS THE ONLY MEANS PETITIONERS HAVE 27

    II. PETITIONERS' RIGHT TO MANDAMUS IS CLEAR AND INDISPUTABLE,........................27

    III. ISSUANCE OF THE WRIT IS APPROPRIATE HERE...29

CONCLUSION..30
CERTIFICATE OF SERVICE/COMPLIANCE.....31
APPENDIX..32

TABLE OF AUTHORITIES

Cases

McClellan v. Carland,
217 U. S. 268, at 269, 280..........................3,4,19

De Beers Consol. Mines, Ltd. v. United States,
325 U.S. 212 4

Beacon Theatres, Inc. v. Westover,
359 U.S. 500, Footnote 16................................5

Frey v. Gangwish, 970 F.2d 1516......................8

United States v. Mellon Bank, N. A.,
545 F.2d 869, 872 (3d Cir. 1976).......................9

Chicot County v. Sherwood, 148 U. S. 529..........10

Johnson v. Bell, 605 F.3d 333, 339....................12

US Court of Appeals for the D.C. Circuit
463 F.2d 268...14

Pennoyer v. Neff, 95 U. S. 714, at
732..17,23

Toucey v. New York Life Insurance Co.,
314 U.S. 118, at 135 2,5

Marshall v. Holmes, 141 U.S.
589..2,6

Simon v. Southern Railway Co., 236 U.S. 115..27

Essanay Film Co. v. Kane, 258 U.S. 358..27

Atchison, T. & S.F.R. Co. v. Wells, 265 U.S. 101 27

Wells Fargo & Co. v. Taylor, 254 U.S. 175...........27

In re Lombardi, 741 F.3d 888, 893 quoting MohawkIndus., Inc. v. Carpenter, 558 U.S. 100, 111 (2009)...................................30

CONSTITUTIONAL PROVISIONS, AND STATUTES AT ISSUE

The First, Fourth, Fifth, Seventh, Ninth, Tenth, and Fourteenth Amendments To The United States Constitution.............15,16,17,20

42 U.S. Code § 1983 and § 1985....................2,4,5,6

15 U.S. Code § 1692 et seq................................2

28 U.S.C. § 1651(a) and 28 U.S.C. § 1254(1)...3,5,28

Constitutional Provisions and Statutes are reprinted in its entirety in the appendix pages 106-9.

OPINIONS BELOW

The order of the United States Court of Appeals for the Sixth Circuit denying rehearing *en banc* was filed on November 14 2018.[1] The order of the United States Court of Appeals for the Sixth Circuit denying this appeal was filed on September 13, 2018.[2] The Notice of Appeal to the Sixth Circuit was filed on February 7, 2018. The memorandum order of the United States District Court for the dismissal of the complaint was filed on January 9, 2018.[3] All of which is reprinted in the Appendix hereto, pages 32-105.

JURISDICTION

On February 16, 2016, petitioners filed the instant case in the United States District Court for the Eastern Division of Tennessee at Knoxville.[4] We

---

[1] Appeal No. 18-5146, DOC 27

[2] Appeal No. 18-5146, DOC 24

[3] Case No. 3:16-cv-00078, DOC 66

alleged, inter alia, deprivations of our civil and equal rights within the meaning Title 42 § 1983 and § 1985 and violations of the Fair Debt Collection Practices Act, 15 U.S. Code § 1692 et seq. On March 28, 2017, the District Court dismissed petitioners §§1983 & 1985 claims.[5] On January 9, 2018, the district court dismissed the remaining original FDCPA claim, while sending a second FDCPA claim which arose during federal court litigation to the state court.[6] On February 7, 2018, the petitioners timely filed an appeal with the United States Circuit Court of Appeals for the Sixth Circuit, which affirmed the district court's ruling on September 13, 2018.[7] On October 11, 2018 Petitioners timely filed a petition for rehearing en banc with the Sixth -

---

[4] Case No. 3:16—cv-00078

[5] Case No. 3:16-cv-00078, DOC 28

[6] Case No. 3:16-cv-00078, DOC 66

[7] Appeal No. 18-5146, DOC 24

Circuit,[8] which was denied on November 14, 2018.[9] Petitioners have timely filed this Petition and the jurisdiction of this Court to review the Judgment of the Sixth Circuit is invoked under 28 U.S.C. § 1651(a) or 28 U.S.C. § 1254(1).

STANDARD OF REVIEW

This Court has authority under the All Writs Act to issue writs of mandamus to the court of appeals in order to prevent its appellate jurisdiction from being thwarted, or defeated by the unauthorized action of the court below.[10] This action is ripe for mandamus intervention by this Court because it involves petitioner's rights under the federal constitution and statutory rights under the FDCPA. An official act of the district court is in contravention of a constitutional and statutory duty, not merely a

---

[8] Appeal No. 18-5146, DOC 26

[9] Appeal No. 18-5146, DOC 27

[10] McClellan v. Carland, 217 U. S. 268, at 269

discretion of authority.[11] The grant of mandamus is therefore an equitable remedy; a matter for the discretion of the court, the exercise of which is governed by well-settled principles.[12]

RELIEF SOUGHT

Petitioners William Kinney and Margaret Kinney respectfully request that the Court grant this petition for a writ of mandamus and direct the district court to (1) reinstate petitioner's claims under Title 42 §§ 1983 and 1985, (2) reinstate petitioner's claims under the FDCPA, and (3) compel the respondents to comply with all district court

---

[11] De Beers Consol. Mines, Ltd. v. United States, 325 U.S. 212 '[the court] took some action it was not empowered to take or declined to take some action required of it." See also Roche v. Evaporated Milk Ass'n, 319 U.S. 21, at 26, "The traditional use of the writ in aid of appellate jurisdiction both at common law and in the federal courts has been to confine an inferior court to a lawful exercise of its prescribed jurisdiction or to compel it to exercise its authority when it is its duty to do so."

[12] McClellan v. Carland, 217 U.S. 268, at 280.

orders still pending, and (4) to promptly rule on Petitioner's long pending motions in federal court further stated herein, including petitioner's unopposed Urgent Motion to Enjoin the State Court Proceedings filed with the Sixth Circuit that was unanswered in its review. 42 U.S.C. § 1983 vests federal courts with the power to enjoin a person acting under color of state law from depriving a United States citizen of any rights, privileges, or immunities secured by the Constitution and laws of the United States. Injunctive relief is also authorized by § 4 of the Sherman Act. [DOC 59] Petitioners civil and equal rights have suffered, and continue to suffer, irreparable harm and inadequacy of legal remedies. [Beacon Theatres, Inc. v. Westover, 359 U.S. 500, at 506, 507] We have been improperly denied a jury trial, and mandamus is available under the All Writs Act, 28 U.S.C. § 1651. [359 U.S. 511]

INTRODUCTION

Unless otherwise stated, all references to court documents are for Case No. 3:16-cv-00078, which is Appeal No. 18-5146. On February 16, 2016, Petitioners filed a claim in the U.S. District Court in Knoxville, Tennessee, for the Eastern Division of Tennessee, the Honorable Chief Judge Thomas A. Varlan, presiding. Our Complaint stated violations of our civil and equal rights within the meaning of Title 42 §§ 1983 and 1985, as well as violations of the Fair Debt Collection Practices Act, Title 15 Section § 1692 et seq. On March 28, 2017, the district court dismissed our § § 1983 and 1985 claim. On January 9, 2018, the court dismissed the Petitioner's FDCPA claim as barred by the statute of limitations, while pending before the court, there was a new FDCPA claim that was not barred by the statute of limitations. The court dismissed this case without ruling on motions related to discovery fraud and Fraud Upon the Court that invoked equitable tolling of the FDCPA statute of limitations under the

Doctrine of Fraudulent concealment and Fraud Upon the Court. The District Court's order violates Petitioners' constitutionally protected right to due process.[13] The Order exceeds the district court's authority and proper judicial role in that the court has refused to exercise its functions. If ever the extraordinary remedy of a writ of mandamus is warranted, it is here. The district court's order must be vacated.[14]

---

[13] Denial of a litigant's right to trial before the court amounts to an abdication of judicial function and is an abuse of discretion. [La Buy v. Howes Leather Co., Inc., 352 U.S. 249, at 256] This Court's mandamus practice is "necessary to protect the constitutional right to trial by jury." [Kamen v. Nordberg, 485 U.S. 939, 940]   "[t]he right of trial by jury as declared by the Seventh Amendment to the Constitution or as given by a statute of the United States shall be preserved . . . inviolate." [Beacon Theatres, Inc. v. Westover, 359 U.S. 500, Footnote 16.]

[14] Included in the Order dismissing Petitioner's Section 1983 claim was a Rule 5.1 Constitutional Challenge of Tennessee's law for the unlicensed practice of (UPL), and a Motion to Enjoin Tennessee's UPL law for violating the Sherman Anti-Trust Act. These two items have been presented separately to this court in a Petition for a Writ of Certiorari filed on or about February 12, 2019.

ARGUMENT

1. The FDCPA claim of April 10, 2017, or "new FDCPA claim."

Respondent Anderson's original state claim is against the petitioners only. On April 10, 2017, respondent Anderson initiated a new and discrete unlawful debt collection activity against the "Kinney Family," [15] that violates Sections 1692(d-g) of the FDCPA and is not barred by the statute of limitations. Petitioners disputed the debt, and respondent Anderson provided no validation notice.[16] Respondents state the alleged debt is from

---

[15] DOC 32 Page ID #: 506. Also, DOC 35-3, Page ID #: 584, item No. 4., Also, DOC 35-3, Page 13 of 25 (No Page ID # was assigned). This dismissal conflicts with the Congressional intent of the FDCPA to protect "Another group of people who do not owe money but may be deliberately harassed...the family...of the consumer." H.R. Rep. No. 131, at 8

[16] Frey v. Gangwish, 970 F.2d 1516 (6th Cir. 1992)

a commercial account, however, when directed by the district court to produce said commercial credit contract executed by the petitioners, the respondents failed to do so. Neither the district court or the Appeals Court had the discretionary authority to deny the petitioners a federal right of action and benefit of a trial concerning the new FDCPA claim.[17] In its order for dismissal, the district court mischaracterized the new FDCPA claim as a "state law claim."[18] This court has stated that "A federal court cannot abandon its jurisdiction already properly obtained of a suit and turn the matter over for adjudication to the state court," which is

---

[17] To satisfy the jurisdictional prerequisite, it is not necessary that a case be pending in the court asked to issue the writ. Rather, it suffices that the case may at some future time come within the court's appellate jurisdiction. See, e. g., United States v. Mellon Bank, N. A., 545 F.2d 869, 872 (3d Cir. 1976).

[18] "…Plaintiff's FDCPA claims will be dismissed, and the remaining claims are state law claims…" No.78, Document 66, Page ID #: 1173

precisely what has occurred in this case.[19] By dismissing the new FDCPA claim, the district court has prevented this controversy from being adjudicated and has thereby defeated appellate review.[20] Subsequently, the subject matter of the district court's action is within the appellate jurisdiction of this court for purposes of the All Writs Act.

2. Petitioner's Original FDCPA Claim, and Tolling the Statute of Limitation for Fraud Upon the Court

At a hearing held at the District Court in Knoxville, TN, on October 18, 2017, the HONORABLE H. Bruce Guyton, Chief Magistrate Judge for the Eastern Division of Tennessee, asked respondent Anderson to produce the Anderson

---

[19] Chicot County v. Sherwood, 148 U. S. 529

[20] UNITED STATES of America v. Hon. Judge Almeric L. Christian, 660 F.2d 892, at 12

<u>Lumber credit contract</u> allegedly executed by the petitioners, which is the account sued upon in the state case.[21] When the respondent could not produce such a document at said hearing, Judge Guyton asked respondent Anderson's counsel; "Counsel, do you have a completed, filled-out, signed Anderson Lumber Company credit application from any of these parties? Atty. Melanie E. Davis (Kizer & Black) told the court, **"There's a copy of it somewhere around the office."** Atty. Morton responded: **"To my knowledge, Your Honor, there was, but I don't have it here in front of me to actually confirm."**[22] Both statements made by Atty. Davis and Atty. Morton were judicial admissions made to Judge Guyton to assert the truth of a matter. Namely that the Anderson Lumber credit application not only exists, it is located somewhere at the law office of Kizer &

---

[21] Case No. 3:16-cv-00078, DOC 54, Page ID # 1058 (The Court Order to Produce)

[22] Case No. 3:16-cv-00078, DOC 71, Transcript Page 33, lines 9-16]

Black.²³ Both statements were false representations intentionally made to conceal Petitioner's right of action, and prevent the court from learning that respondent Anderson lacks standing to bring the state lawsuit. The respondent's attack upon the fundamental fairness and integrity of the court constitutes Fraud Upon the Court which has no Statute of Limitations.²⁴ The Doctrine of Fraudulent Concealment and Equitable tolling apply to Petitioner's original FDCPA claim (Case No. 00078).

3. Fraudulent Concealment and Equitable Tolling

Pursuant to F.R.C.P., Rule 72(a); and Rule 28

---

[23] Appeal No. 18-5150, DOC 11-1, Page 25

[24] Johnson v. Bell, 605 F.3d 333, 339 (6th Cir. 2010) See also US Court of Appeals for the District of Columbia Circuit - 463 F.2d 268 (D.C. Cir. 1971) "The spirit of the "fraud on the court" rule is applicable whenever the integrity of the judicial process or functioning has been undercut--certainly in any instance of misconduct by a party."

U.S. Code § 636(b)(1)(C), on January 5, 2018, petitioners timely filed a Motion to Reconsider [DOC 65] Magistrate Judge Guyton's Memorandum and Order [DOC 54]. Judge Guyton erroneously denied our Motion to Compel for non-compliance with a scheduling order, although the petitioners provided the court with a certified letter showing that we did comply with the scheduling order. [Case 3:16-cv-00078, DOC 65-1, Page ID #: 1164] Petitioner's Motion to Compel was a request to compel the respondents to furnish copies of the documents that form the legal basis for their state claim, and are also relevant and material to petitioners FDCPA claim. These are the same documents the district court ordered the respondents to produce - **to no avail**. [Doc 54, Page ID #: 1058] In said motion to reconsider, the petitioners further demonstrated to the court the existence of a multitude of deceptive responses and non-answers made by the respondents to fraudulently conceal the factual predicate of petitioner's claim. Petitioner's moved for sanctions pursuant to F.R.C.P., Rule 16(f)(C) for failure to comply with pre-trial orders, and contempt charges pursuant to Rule 11. Petitioners also requested relief pursuant to Rule 37(b)(2)(A)(i), that the court accept as established for the purposes of this action, that the respondents will not or cannot produce the documents it was ordered to produce by the court. [DOC 65, Page ID #: 1160]. Petitioner would then move to toll the statute of limitations under the doctrine of Equitable Tolling on the grounds of Fraudulent concealment and Fraud Upon the Court. However four days later, on January 9, 2018, the district court improvidently dismissed our claim without ruling on said motions. [FDIC v. Morriss, 273 F. App'x 390, 390-391 (5th Cir. 2008) "A district court abuses its discretion when it . . . ignores or misunderstands the relevant evidence, and bases its decision upon considerations having little factual support."]

Furthermore, on January 9, 2018, petitioners mailed to the district court a request for a hearing to resolve discovery disputes [DOC 68], that was received on January 11, 2018, (USPS Certified Mail No. 7005 1160 0004 5533 2697), but not filed until January 23, 2018. Document #68 further detailed the defendant's discovery abuse (and fraud), and also addressed numerous instances whereby the district court <u>constrained the petitioners</u> in their attempts at discovery. Plaintiffs have not been accorded an opportunity for full and fair litigation.

4. Petitioners Challenge of State Court Jurisdiction

Jurisdiction can only be conferred by law. In our initial and amended pleadings we challenged the state court's unlawful jurisdiction which violates our rights under the due process clause of the Fourteenth Amendment[25] While TN Code 16-10-101

---

[25] Case 3:16-cv-00078, DOC 1, Filed 02/16/16, Page ID #: 12. Also DOC 58, Page ID # 108, Paragraph 22.

confers general jurisdiction on the state's circuit courts, Tennessee's Supreme Court requires the plaintiff to make a prima facie showing in order for the state to exercise jurisdiction over a defendant that comports with the 14th Amendment.[26] Respondents filed a fraudulent claim in state court that does not invoke the jurisdiction of the court, but the state court has proceeded anyway.[27] When the respondents were ordered by the district court to produce documents material as to whether or not the state court has lawful jurisdiction over the petitioners, the respondents ignored the district court's order without consequence, and our federal complaint was dismissed.[28] This court ruled in

---

[26] Appeal No. 18-5150, DOCUMENT 11-1 Pages 18-27.

[27] Anderson Lumber Company, Inc. v. Kinney et al, Blount County Circuit Court, Case No. E-24747

[28] [DOC 54] 25 Am.Jur., Habeas Corpus, sec. 27, p. 161. See also Palmer v. Ashe, supra. "Jurisdiction of the person and of the subject matter is not alone conclusive [and] the jurisdiction of the court to make or render the order or judgment" depends upon due observance of the constitutional rights of the accused.

Pennoyer that "the judgment of a court lacking personal jurisdiction violate[s] the Due Process Clause of the Fourteenth Amendment,"[29] and "The requirement that a court have personal jurisdiction flows not from Art. III, but from the Due Process Clause: the personal jurisdiction requirement recognizes and protects an individual liberty interest. It represents a restriction on judicial power not as a matter of sovereignty, but as a matter of individual liberty." [Ins. Co. of Ireland v. Compagnie Des Bauxites, 456 U.S. 694 at 702] Petitioners implicitly state and can affirmatively demonstrate that the state court does not have subject matter or personal jurisdiction over the petitioners. The dismissal of Case No. 00078 [DOC 28] before the matter of lawful state court jurisdiction was resolved, has in effect reduced the Petitioners to the state of having no legal status.

---

[29] *Pennoyer v. Neff,* 95 U. S. 714, 95 U. S. 732 (1878), "the judgment of a court lacking personal jurisdiction violated the Due Process Clause of the Fourteenth Amendment as well."

This is the principle truth of the matter, we have not been accorded our constitutional rights by the district court or the Sixth Circuit.

5. Revised Amended Complaint

On May 25, 2017, for the first time since filing our initial complaint on February 16, 2016, petitioners filed a motion for leave of court to amend their complaint [DOC 35]. While there had yet to be a ruling on DOC 35, petitioners filed a revised amended complaint on December 5, 2017[30] to include new unlawful actions taken by the

---

[30] The revised amended complaint [DOC 58] included the new FDCPA Claim, Page 1084, the issue of UPL and the Sherman Anti-Trust Act, Page ID # 1084, the State Court Jurisdictional Issue, Page ID # 1085, the issue of Fraud Upon the Court, Page ID # 1093, and the Ex Parte hearing held on June 12, 2017 at state court.

respondents. Petitioners revised amended complaint [DOC 58] superseded DOC 35 and was controlling. The refusal of the trial court to address the violations of our statutory and constitutional rights found in our revised amended complaint in reality and effect, was a refusal to permit the case to come to a hearing upon questions of law and of fact, and "falls little short of a refusal to permit the enforcement of the law." [Ex Parte United States, 287 U.S. 241, at 250] It is established that A Writ of Mandamus may issue in aid of this court's appellate jurisdiction over an unauthorized action of the court below. [McClellan v. Carland, 217 U.S. 268] The Sixth Circuit, in affirming the district court's order, failed to give full legal effect to petitioners revised amended complaint which constitutes an application of unauthorized judicial discretion.

6. Urgent Motion To Stay State Court Proceedings

For the reasons previously stated in Sections 1 and 3 above, and described in our appeals, respondent's fraudulent state claim failed to meet the state standard for acquiring jurisdiction over the petitioners that comports with the Fourteenth Amendment, thus making the state case an unlawful state action against the petitioners which should have been dismissed by the district court. In the absence of a dismissal, petitioners tried unsuccessfully to obtain a Stay from the Appeals Court on the grounds of unlawful state court jurisdiction and the holding of *ex parte* state court hearings that violated petitioner's rights under the due process clause and equal protection clause of the Fourteenth Amendment. Congress enacted 28 U.S.C. § 2283 as an immediately enforceable right, so that persons who have been deprived of federal constitutional rights would not have to endure a state court trial in a tainted setting. In its Order of March 28, 2017, the District Court ruled that petitioners unopposed Motion to Enjoin the State Court Proceedings [DOC 26, Page ID #: 442] was not ripe for consideration. Less than four months later, on June 12, 2017 the respondents and the state court held an *ex parte* hearing and dismissed Petitioner Margaret Kinney's original counterclaim which contained a substantive due process property interest in the form of compensatory damages. On July 6, 2017 petitioners removed the state case to district court for deprivation of civil rights within the meaning of Section 1983. [31] On January 9, 2018, the district court remanded the case without ruling on the June 12, 2017 state hearing, which formed the basis for removal. On June 8, 2018, Petitioners then filed a civil rights claim regarding said June 12, 2017 hearing.[32] On September 6, 2018, petitioners filed an Urgent Motion to Stay the State Court Proceedings with the Sixth Circuit [DOC 23] which was time sensitive. In February of 2018 the respondents had set a state trial date for October 16, 2018, (which was continued by the respondents on

---

[31] Case No. 3:17-cv-00288

[32] Case No. 3:18-cv-00227

September 18, 2018). Petitioner's Urgent Motion for a Stay was based in part on the respondent's refusal to comply with the district court's order to produce documents that are relevant and material to the petitioner's defense in state court. On September 18, 2018, the respondents and the state court held yet another *ex parte* hearing to dismiss William Kinney and Christopher Kinney's counterclaims. Christopher Kinney, an original defendant in the state case, passed away on December 28, 2015. Previously, on April 8, **2016**, in violation of the federal removal statute (28 U.S. Code § 1446(d)) and the Supremacy clause of the U.S. Constitution (Article VI paragraph 2), respondent Anderson held an *ex parte* hearing at state court and obtained an order for non-suit of Christopher Kinney while the district court had jurisdiction. [Case No 3:15-cv-00324, DOC 16] and in complete disregard of the fact that we had filed a motion with the district court to substitute William Kinney for Christopher Kinney. [Case No 3:15-cv-00324, DOC 15]. The *ex parte* hearing of April 8, **2016**, as well as the *ex parte* hearings held on June 12, **2017,** and September 18, **2018,** demonstrate that the state judicial proceedings in question are themselves an independent violation of our federal constitutional rights. The Sixth Circuit did not rule on our motion for a stay. The respondents have demonstrated malice and reckless disregard toward the petitioner's federal constitutional rights.[33] It is beyond dispute that federal courts have jurisdiction over suits such as this, to enjoin state officials from interfering with federal rights.[34] [*Ex parte Young,* 209 U. S. 123, at 160-162]

---

[33] At the time of this writing, Petitioners are in the process of filing supplemental and amended pleadings in Case No. 3;18-cv-00227 to include the ex parte state hearing of September 18, 2018, and a "Class of One" claim. [Case No. 3;18-cv-00227, DOC 28]

[34] This court ruled in *Pennoyer,* "Since the adoption of the Fourteenth Amendment to the Federal Constitution, the validity of such judgments may be directly questioned, and their enforcement in the State resisted, on the ground that proceedings in a court of justice to determine the personal rights and obligations of parties over whom that court has no jurisdiction do not constitute due process of law." Pennoyer v. Neff, 95 U.S. 714, at 733

7. Judicial Notice of Case No. 3:18-cv-00227

When deciding our appeal and Urgent Motion for a Stay of the State Court Proceedings, we requested that the appeals court take notice of Case No. 3:18-cv-00227 filed by petitioners on June 8, 2018, concerning the *ex parte* hearing held by the respondents on June 12, 2017. The state court's issuance (at said hearing) of an immediately enforceable judgment that applied state law to deprive the plaintiffs of a federal right, constitutes state action and thus action under color of state law within the meaning of Title 42 Section 1983. The taking of Margaret's Property unquestionably constitutes a seizure under the Fourth Amendment. The *ex parte* hearing held on June 12, 2017 at state court was in effect, a Quasi In Rem proceeding directed against Petitioner Margaret Kinney's property interest found in her counterclaim (worth approximately $12,000.). The state unlawfully disposed of Margaret's property without providing adequate notice and an opportunity to be heard. This is not a matter of jurisdiction over property properly acquired by the state court. This is property acquired by fraud, in violation of Margaret's federal rights and this court has jurisdiction over the res.[35] The district court must vacate the state court's unlawful order, and enjoin the state court proceeding until the matter of state court jurisdiction is resolved. Petitioner's currently have a Motion for a Show Cause Order pending in the District Court that will resolve the matter of state court jurisdiction with certainty, in favor of the petitioners. [Case No. 3:18-cv-00227] In the meantime, an injunction is necessary in aid of this

---

[35] The rule has become well settled, therefore, that Section 265 does not preclude the use of the injunction by a federal court to restrain state proceedings seeking to interfere with property in the custody of the court. Toucey v. New York Life Insurance Co., 314 U.S. 118, at 135 [See also Footnote 6] *Farmers Loan & Trust Co. v. Lake Street R. Co.*, 177

court's jurisdiction to preserve the court's authority over the res that is the subject of both federal and state litigation. Petitioners Section 1983 claim (found in Case No. 3:18-cv-00227) also authorizes an exception to the anti-injunction act that will end the continued deprivation of petitioner's civil rights from *ex parte* state court hearings until the Show Cause hearing requested by the petitioners can be held in district court. [36]

---

[36] Another group of cases is said to constitute an exception to 265, namely, where federal courts have enjoined litigants from enforcing judgments fraudulently obtained in the state courts. [Marshall v. Holmes, 141 U.S. 589 , 12 S.Ct. 62; Simon v. Southern Railway Co., 236 U.S. 115, 35 S.Ct. 255; Essanay Film Co. v. Kane, 258 U.S. 358 , 42 S.Ct. 318; Atchison, T. & S.F.R. Co. v. Wells, 265 U.S. 101, 44 S.Ct. 469; Wells Fargo & Co. v. Taylor, 254 U.S. 175 , 41 S.Ct. 93.]

REASONS TO GRANT THIS WRIT

I. A WRIT OF MANDAMUS IS THE ONLY MEANS PETITIONERS HAVE TO REMEDY THE IRREPARABLE HARM CAUSED BY THE DISMISSAL OF CASE NO. 3:16-cv-00078.

There can be no real dispute that Petitioners "have no . . . adequate means to attain the relief" they seek other than through mandamus.

II. PETITIONERS' RIGHT TO MANDAMUS IS CLEAR AND INDISPUTABLE.

Petitioners' right to mandamus here is clear and indisputable for the Order exceeds the district court's authority, in that the court has refused to exercise its functions and jurisdiction.

1. Respondents discovery fraud and Fraud Upon the Court, clearly defined in Documents 65 and 68, tolls the statute of limitations on

petitioner's original FDCPA claim under the Doctrine of Equitable Tolling, and was not subject to dismissal.

2. Petitioners had stated a new FDCPA claim from an unlawful debt collection activity initiated by the respondent on April 10, 2017 that was not barred by the statute of limitations. Petitioners were denied a federal right of action.

3. Petitioners Section 1983 claims were not subject to dismissal under Rule 12(b)(6) or Rule 12(c) because the respondent had no right to bring such a motion. The respondents filed a fraudulent claim and the state court clearly does not have jurisdiction over the Kinneys. The District Court's refusal to exercise its functions and address the matter of state court jurisdiction has in effect granted authority to the state court to proceed in violation of the petitioner's federal constitutional and statutory rights

4. The state court proceedings must be stayed under 28 U.S.C. § 1651 or 28 U.S. Code §

2283 until the respondents (1) comply with all district court orders, and (2) the matter of state court jurisdiction is resolved.

III. ISSUANCE OF THE WRIT IS APPROPRIATE HERE

Petitioners clearly satisfy the first two requirements for issuance of a writ. Even once these factors are satisfied, however, "the issuing court, in the exercise of its discretion, must be satisfied that the writ is appropriate under the circumstances." As stated in Section II above, Petitioners have a clear and indisputable right to a ruling on mandamus because the trial court has abused its discretion and the Sixth Circuit Court of Appeals Court has declined to make its own review of the issues stated in this petition. The extraordinary writ of mandamus is a useful safety valve for "promptly correcting serious errors" such as those named in this petition. [In re Lombardi, 741 F.3d 888, 893 (8th Cir. en banc), quoting Mohawk Indus., Inc. v. Carpenter, 558 U.S. 100, 111 (2009).]

CONCLUSION

We have been denied our constitutional and statutory rights in a post judgment appeal. Therefore, this court's ruling in *Roche* to deny mandamus is not applicable because "adequate relief cannot be obtained in any other form from any other court." Petitioners have, in good faith, followed all the required avenues for redress of its injuries prior to respectfully petitioning this Court to grant a writ of mandamus. Submitted this 5th day of February, 2019:

_____
William Kinney

_____
Margaret Kinney

CERTIFICATE OF COMPLIANCE

I certify that this brief is in compliance with the Rules of the Supreme Court of the United States, and contains 4,364 words, excluding the table of contents, table of authorities, Constitutional provisions and statutes, rules or regulations, appendix, and certificate of service.

CERTIFICATE OF SERVICE

A copy of this document has been sent to the respondents, via USPS Certified Mail;

McDonald, Levy, & Taylor; Attorneys at Law, and counsel for Anderson.

10805 Kingston Pike Suite #200

Knoxville, TN 37934

CERTIFIED MAIL RECEIPT NO. – 7018 0360 0000 7989 1643

Kizer & Black, Attorneys, PLLC, and counsel for Anderson.

217 East Broadway Avenue

Maryville, TN 37804

CERTIFIED MAIL RECEIPT NO. – 7018 0360 0000 7989 1636

APPENDIX

Order Denying En Banc Review

Appeal No. 18-5146, DOC 27, filed on November 14, 2018.

UNITED STATES COURT OF APPEALS FOR THE SIXTH CIRCUIT.

WILLIAM KINNEY; MARGARET KINNEY, Plaintiffs-Appellants,

v. ANDERSON LUMBER COMPANY, INC., ET AL., Defendants-Appellees.

O R D E R BEFORE: COLE, Chief Judge; SUHRHEINRICH and THAPAR, Circuit Judges. The court received a petition for rehearing en banc. The original panel has reviewed the petition for rehearing and concludes that the issues raised in the petition were fully considered upon the original submission and decision of the case. The petition then was circulated to the full court. No judge has requested a vote on the suggestion for rehearing en banc. Therefore, the petition is denied. ENTERED BY ORDER OF THE COURT Deborah S. Hunt, Clerk

Order Denying Appeal

Appeal No. 18-5146, DOC 24, filed on September 13, 2018.

UNITED STATES COURT OF APPEALS FOR THE SIXTH CIRCUIT.

WILLIAM KINNEY; MARGARET KINNEY, Plaintiffs-Appellants,

v. ANDERSON LUMBER COMPANY, INC., et al., Defendants-Appellees.

ON APPEAL FROM THE UNITED STATES DISTRICT COURT FOR THE EASTERN DISTRICT OF TENNESSEE O R D E R Before: COLE, Chief Judge; SUHRHEINRICH and THAPAR, Circuit Judges.

William and Margaret Kinney, Tennessee residents proceeding pro se, appeal the district court's judgment granting the defendants' separate dispositive motions filed under Rules 12(b)(6) and 12(c) of the Federal Rules of Civil Procedure. This case has been referred to a panel of the court that, upon examination, unanimously agrees that oral argument is not needed. See Fed. R. App. P. 34(a). In 2012, Anderson Lumber Company, Inc., ("Anderson Lumber") sued Christopher and

Margaret Kinney, d/b/a/ Kinney Custom Interiors, in Tennessee state court. Anderson Lumber's lawsuit sought to recover a debt that the Kinneys allegedly owed for "supplies and materials" they had purchased. William Kinney subsequently intervened as a defendant in the lawsuit. The trial judge referred the case to Special Master Jason Rose who, after holding a hearing on the matter, issued a report concluding that the Kinneys owed Anderson Lumber $32,912.95. The Kinneys tried removing the lawsuit to federal court during the pendency of the case, but the district court ultimately remanded the matter to state court. See Anderson Lumber Co. v. Kinney, No. E2016-01640-COA-T10B-CV, 2016 WL 6248597, at *1-2 (Tenn. Ct. App. Oct. 26, 2016). In February 2016, while Anderson Lumber's state lawsuit was still ongoing, William and Margaret Kinney filed this federal lawsuit. The Kinneys' complaint, which they later amended, named the following defendants: Anderson Lumber; Anderson Lumber's attorneys, Kizer & Black Attorneys, PLLC, and McDonald, Levy & Taylor, P.C.;

Anderson Lumber's financial company, Blue Tarp Financial, Inc.; and Special Master Rose. The Kinneys alleged that some of the defendants falsely represented that the Kinneys owed a debt that was not authorized by any agreement, in violation of the Fair Debt Collection Practices Act ("FDCPA"), 15 U.S.C. § 1692, et seq. They also alleged that Anderson Lumber's state lawsuit violated § 1692f of the Act, and that Anderson Lumber's request for attorney's fees in the state lawsuit constituted a violation of § 1692i(a)(2)(A). Additionally, the Kinneys alleged that some of the defendants "reopened Margaret's account without her permission, and applied five invoices that were forgeries (totaling $16,498.72)" in violation of the Electronic Fund Transfer Act, 15 U.S.C. § 1693, et seq. They further alleged that some of the defendants violated Margaret Kinney's privacy rights as codified in 15 U.S.C. § 6821 (Privacy Protection for Customer Information of Financial Institutions) by obtaining the credit application that she allegedly executed. Finally, the Kinneys alleged several instances where they were denied their constitutional rights during the course of the state lawsuit, in violation of 42 U.S.C. §§ 1983 and 1985. They sought compensatory and punitive damages, as well as court costs and attorney's fees. The defendants all filed separate Rule 12(b)(6) motions to dismiss the Kinneys' complaint for failing to state a claim upon which relief can be granted, arguing that the Kinneys' claims were, among other things, barred by the applicable statutes of limitations, Tennessee's litigation privilege, or the doctrine of absolute judicial immunity. The Kinneys opposed the defendants' Rule 12(b)(6) motions and also sought leave to file an amended complaint. In ruling upon the various motions to dismiss, the district court denied the Kinneys leave to amend their complaint and dismissed all of their claims, save for their FDCPA claims against Anderson Lumber; McDonald, Levy & Taylor, P.C.; and Kizer & Black Attorneys, PLLC. Anderson Lumber; McDonald, Levy & Taylor, P.C.; and Kizer & Black Attorneys, PLLC, thereafter filed separate Rule 12(c) motions for judgment on the pleadings, in which they argued, among other things, that the Kinneys' FDCPA claims were barred by the applicable statute of limitations. The Kinneys opposed the defendants' motions and again moved for leave to amend their complaint. The district court denied the Kinneys' second motion for leave to amend, granted the defendants' Rule 12(c) motions on the basis that the Kinneys' FDCPA claims were time-barred, and entered judgment for the defendants. The Kinneys filed this timely appeal. The Kinneys advance five principal arguments for our review. First, they contend that the district court erred by granting the defendants' Rule 12(b)(6) motions with respect to their 42 U.S.C. § 1983 claims. Second, they argue that the district court erred by denying their second motion for leave to amend their complaint. Third, they argue that the district court erred by dismissing their claims during factual development when the court "knew, or should have known, based on documentary and testimonial evidence," that the defendants had committed discovery fraud and fraud upon the court. Fourth, they argue that the district court erred by granting the defendants' Rule 12(c) motions with respect to their FDCPA claims. And at the outset, the Kinneys claim that the district court erred by not enjoining Anderson Lumber's civil lawsuit in Tennessee state court. The Anti-Injunction Act, 28 U.S.C. § 2283, prohibits federal courts from enjoining a state-court proceeding unless it is expressly authorized by statute or it is necessary to aid in the federal court's jurisdiction or to protect or effectuate its judgments. Because none of those exceptions applies here, the Kinneys' argument on this point is meritless. I. Motions to Dismiss The Kinneys first challenge the district court's order granting the defendants' Rule 12(b)(6) motions, but solely with respect to their § 1983 claims. We review de novo the district court's dismissal of a complaint under Rule 12(b)(6). See Tackett v. M & G Polymers,USA, LLC, 561 F.3d 478, 481 (6th Cir. 2009) (citations omitted). A complaint is subject to dismissal Case: 18-5146 Document: 24-1 Filed: 09/13/2018 Page: 3 No. 18-5146 - 4 - under

Rule 12(b)(6) if it fails to plead facts that plausibly state a claim for relief. See Cataldo v. U.S. Steel Corp., 676 F.3d 542, 547 (6th Cir. 2012). When reviewing a Rule 12(b)(6) motion, we must confine our analysis to the pleadings and accept all well-pleaded allegations as true. See Tackett, 561 F.3d at 481. The Kinneys' complaint alleged that at each of the five hearings held "beginning on July 1, 2013, and continuing until the Special Master's hearing on February 13, 2015," the defendants and the state trial judge "deliberately and willfully conspired to deprive [them] of [their constitutional] rights," primarily through the trial judge's adverse rulings on several motions. The Kinneys alleged that, although the defendants are private actors, they "are inexorably linked to the State actions of Judge David R. Duggan, who presided over each one of the five judicial hearings." The Kinneys, however, did not name Judge Duggan as a defendant in the present lawsuit, recognizing that he is entitled to absolute judicial immunity. The district court determined that the Kinneys failed to state a claim upon which relief could be granted because they did not sufficiently allege that the defendants conspired with Judge Duggan to deprive them of any federally protected right. The district court further concluded that Special Master Rose was entitled to absolute judicial immunity. To state a claim under 42 U.S.C. § 1983, a plaintiff must show that he or she was deprived of a right secured by the Constitution or laws of the United States and that the deprivation was at the hands of a person acting under the color of state law. Flagg Bros. v. Brooks, 436 U.S. 149, 155 (1978); Memphis, Tenn. Area Local, Am. Postal Workers Union v. City of Memphis, 361 F.3d 898, 905 (6th Cir. 2004). Section 1983 is not a vehicle for proceeding against a private party "'no matter how discriminatory or wrongful' the party's conduct." Tahfs v. Proctor, 316 F.3d 584, 590 (6th Cir. 2003) (quoting Am. Mfrs. Mut. Ins. Co. v. Sullivan, 526 U.S. 40, 50 (1999)). However, private persons, by their actions, can become state actors for purposes of liability under § 1983. Adickes v. S.H. Kress & Co., 398 U.S. 144, 152 (1970). That is, private persons may be held liable under § 1983 if they willfully participate in joint activity with state agents. City of Memphis, 361 F.3d at 905. Thus, because most of the defendants are private entities, the Kinneys must prove that Anderson Lumber; Kizer & Black Attorneys, PLLC; McDonald, Levy & Taylor, P.C.; and Blue Tarp Financial, Inc., all conspired with the state trial judge to deprive them of their constitutional rights. The standard for proving civil conspiracy is as follows: A civil conspiracy is an agreement between two or more persons to injure another by unlawful action. Express agreement among all the conspirators is not necessary to find the existence of a civil conspiracy. Each conspirator need not have known all of the details of the illegal plan or all of the participants involved. All that must be shown is that there was a single plan, that the alleged coconspirator shared in the general conspiratorial objective, and that an overt act was committed in furtherance of the conspiracy that caused injury to the complainant. Hooks v. Hooks, 771 F.2d 935, 943-44 (6th Cir. 1985). "Although circumstantial evidence may prove a conspiracy, '[i]t is well-settled that conspiracy claims must be pled with some degree of specificity and that vague and conclusory allegations unsupported by material facts will not be sufficient to state such a claim under § 1983." Heyne v. Metro. Nashville Pub. Sch., 655 F.3d 556, 563 (6th Cir. 2011) (alteration in original) (quoting Spadafore v. Gardner, 330 F.3d 849, 854 (6th Cir. 2003)). The Kinneys alleged that the defendants conspired with Judge Duggan to violate their federal rights because Judge Duggan issued several rulings that were adverse to them, yet favorable to the defendants. But such an allegation is merely a legal conclusion that we do not accept as true. See id. at 563-64. The Kinneys' complaint does not contain specific allegations of a plan or agreement between the defendants and the state trial judge to violate their constitutional rights. See Dennis v. Sparks, 449 U.S. 24, 28 (1980) ("[M]erely resorting to the courts and being on the winning side of a lawsuit does not make a party a co-conspirator or a joint actor with the judge."). Additionally, with respect to Special Master Rose, we have recognized that those persons "performing tasks ... integral [to] or intertwined with the judicial process" are accorded quasijudicial immunity. Bush v. Rauch, 38 F.3d 842, 847 (6th Cir. 1994). Judge Duggan assigned Jason Rose to act as the special master. Thus, his actions are cloaked with absolute immunity, even if his actions were in error or done maliciously, because they were nonetheless performed in furtherance of the judicial process. See Stump v. Sparkman, 435 U.S. 349, 356-57 (1978); Nystedt v. Nigro, 700 F.3d 25, 31-32 (1st Cir. 2012). Based on the foregoing, the district court properly granted the defendants' respective Rule 12(b)(6) motions with respect to the Kinneys' § 1983 claims. II. Second Motion to Amend Complaint The Kinneys next argue that the district court erred by denying their second motion for leave to amend their complaint, in which they sought (1) to rename Blue Tarp Financial, Inc., as a defendant on the basis that it had committed FDCPA, and (2) bring other state-law claims against the defendants. The district court provided two bases for denying the Kinneys' motion for leave to amend their complaint. First, the district court determined that permitting the Kinneys to amend their complaint for a second time would have caused "undue prejudice to [the] defendants" and "unnecessary delay." We defer to a district court's view of what equity requires in a specific case, so review of the denial of a motion for leave to amend a complaint is ordinarily for an abuse of discretion. Yuhasz v. Brush Wellman, Inc., 341 F.3d 559, 569 (6th Cir. 2003). Second, the district court denied the motion "on grounds of futility," a decision which we review de novo. See Babcock v. Michigan, 812 F.3d 531, 541 (6th Cir. 2016). An amendment is futile if it could not withstand a Rule 12(b)(6) motion to dismiss. SFS Check, LLC v. First Bank of Del., 774 F.3d 351, 355 (6th Cir. 2014). Although the Federal Rules of Civil Procedure instruct district courts to "freely" grant parties leave to amend "when justice so requires," see Fed. R. Civ. P. 15(a)(2): [a] district court may deny a party leave to amend a complaint if there is "undue delay, bad faith or dilatory motive on the part of the movant, repeated failure to cure deficiencies by amendments previously allowed, undue prejudice to the opposing party by virtue of allowance of the amendment, futility of amendment, etc." Raiser v. Corp. of President of Church of Jesus Christ of Latter-Day Saints, 494 F. App'x 506, 508 (6th Cir. 2012) (quoting Foman v. Davis, 371 U.S. 178, 182 (1962)). Here, the district court appropriately determined that the Kinneys' proposed amendment to their complaint would have been futile. The Kinneys' proposed amended complaint sought to rename Blue Tarp Financial, Inc., as a defendant on the basis that it had committed FDCPA and other state-law violations. However, as discussed below, the district court properly dismissed the Kinneys' FDCPA claims as time-barred. And the district court did not abuse its discretion by declining to exercise supplemental jurisdiction over the new state-law claims between non-diverse parties that the Kinneys' sought to include in their proposed amended complaint. See Hobbs v. Duggins, 318 F. App'x 375, 376 (6th Cir.

2009). Thus, any amendment would have been futile. See Campbell v. BNSF Ry. Co., 600 F.3d 667, 677 (6th Cir. 2010). Because the district court did not err by denying the Kinneys' second motion to amend their complaint on the basis of futility, we need not consider the district court's alternative basis for denying the motion. III. Motions for Judgment on the Pleadings Finally, the Kinneys argue that the district court erred by granting Anderson Lumber; McDonald, Levy & Taylor, P.C.; and Kizer & Black Attorneys, PLLC's Rule 12(c) motions with respect to their FDCPA claims. We review orders granting Rule 12(c) motions for judgment on the pleadings under the same de novo standard applicable to motions to dismiss for failure to state a claim under Rule 12(b)(6). See HDC, LLC v. City of Ann Arbor, 675 F.3d 608, 611 (6th Cir. 2012). In doing so, we view the complaint in the light most favorable to the plaintiff, accepting as true "all plausible well-pled factual allegations," and drawing "all reasonable inferences" in favor of the plaintiff. Lutz v. Chesapeake Appalachia, LLC, 717 F.3d 459,

464 (6th Cir. 2013). In general, a motion for judgment on the pleadings "is an 'inappropriate vehicle' for dismissing a claim based upon a statute of limitations," and we will approve of granting one only if "the allegations in the complaint affirmatively show that the claim is time-barred." Id. (quoting Cataldo, 676 F.3d at 547). An action under the FDCPA must be brought "within one year from the date on which the violation occurs." 15 U.S.C. § 1692k(d). The district court correctly observed that the defendants filed the underlying state-court lawsuit on November 21, 2012, but that the Kinneys did not file the present federal lawsuit until February 16, 2016, well beyond the one-year limitations period. The Kinneys argued below that their FDCPA claims were not time-barred based on the "continuing violations" doctrine. But we have declined to apply that doctrine in the context of the FDCPA. Slorp v. Lerner, Sampson & Rothfuss, 587 F. App'x 249, 257-59 (6th Cir. 2014). The district court properly dismissed the Kinneys' FDCPA claims. IV. Discovery Fraud and Fraud upon the

Court Finally, the Kinneys argue that the district court erred by dismissing their claims where it "knew, or should have known, based on documentary and testimonial evidence," that the defendants had committed discovery fraud and fraud upon the court. However, the Kinneys have forfeited this argument because they did not raise it below. See United States v. Ellison, 462 F.3d 557, 560 (6th Cir. 2006) ("[T]his court generally will not consider an argument not raised in the district court and presented for the first time on appeal."). Accordingly, we AFFIRM the district court's judgment. ENTERED BY ORDER OF THE COURT Deborah S. Hunt, Clerk

Order for Dismissal

Case No. 3:16-cv-0078, DOC 66 , filed January 9, 2018

UNITED STATES DISTRICT COURT - EASTERN DISTRICT OF TENNESSEE William Kinney Margaret Kinney v. ANDERSON LUMBER COMPANY, INC., BLUE TARP FINANCIAL, INC., KIZER & BLACK ATTORNEYS, PLLC.

McDONALD, LEVY, & TAYLOR, P.C., and JASON ROSE.

MEMORANDUM OPINION

Before the Court are plaintiffs' motion for leave to amend the complaint [Docs. 35, 36] and defendants' motions for judgment on the pleadings [Docs. 32, 33, 48]. Defendants responded to plaintiffs' motion [Doc. 38], and plaintiffs responded to defendants' motions [Docs. 34, 37, 50]. Plaintiffs also filed a reply regarding their motion for leave to amend [Doc. 39]. For the reasons explained below, the Court will deny plaintiffs' motion for leave to amend and grant defendants' motions for judgment on the pleadings.

BACKGROUND

This matter originated when defendant Anderson Lumber Company, Inc. ("Anderson") filed a complaint on November 21, 2012, against "Chris Kinney and Margaret Kinney, d/b/a Kinney Custom Interiors," in the Circuit Court for Blount County, Tennessee, Equity Division [Case No. 3:15-cv-324,

Doc. 3 pp. 7–8]. In the complaint underlying the state action, Anderson sought recovery of $34,765.98 from the Kinneys for "supplies and materials" they allegedly purchased from Anderson [*Id.*]. Anderson's corporate attorney, John T. McArthur of the firm Kizer & Black Attorneys, PLLC ("K&B"), filed the state action [*Id.* at 8]. On August 11, 2014, the state court added William Kinney as an additional defendant to the action [*Id.* at 12]. On December 2, 2014, the Circuit Court for Blount County issued an order referring the case to Special Master Jason Rose [Case No. 3:15-cv-324, Doc. 1-2 pp. 85–86]. A hearing was held on February 13, 2015, and Special Master Rose issued a report on April 30, 2015 [3:15-cv-324, Doc. 3 pp. 15–19]. He determined that that the Kinneys owed Anderson $32,912.95 [*Id.*]. On July 28, 2015, the Kinneys attempted to remove the state action to federal court by filing a notice of removal [3:15-cv-324, Doc. 1]. Anderson then filed a motion to remand [3:15-cv-324, Doc. 3], which the Court granted [3:15-cv-324, Docs. 7, 8]. Plaintiffs then once again attempted to remove the underlying state court action to federal court [3:17-cv-288, Doc. 1], and defendants filed motions to remand [3:17-cv288, Docs. 4, 5], which the Court granted [3:17-cv-288, Doc. 12]. On February 16, 2016, plaintiffs, acting *pro se*, filed the present action, alleging a number of claims against Anderson, their lawyers, various finance firms, and Jason Rose, the special master in the state court proceedings [Doc. 1]. Defendants filed motions to dismiss [Docs. 4–7, 14], after which plaintiffs moved for leave to amend the complaint [Doc. 23], which they had previously amended once before [Doc. 3]. On March 28, 2017, the Court granted in part and denied in part defendants' motion to dismiss, allowing only plaintiffs' Fair Debt Collection Practices Act ("FDCPA") claims against Anderson, McDonald, and K&B to proceed [Doc. 28]. The Court also denied plaintiffs' motion to amend the complaint for failure to comply with local rules, undue delay in moving to amend, and futility [*Id.*]. The remaining defendants then filed motions for judgment on the pleadings [Docs. 32, 33, 48], after which plaintiffs again moved for leave to amend the complaint [Docs. 35, 36]. These motions are presently before the Court.

ANALYSIS

Although plaintiffs filed their motion to amend after defendants filed their motions for judgment on the pleadings, granting a motion for judgment on the pleadings before addressing a pending motion to amend can be an abuse of discretion. *See Thompson v. Superior Fireplace Co.*, 931 F.2d 372, 374 (6th Cir. 1991). As such, the Court first considers plaintiffs' motion to amend, and will then turn to defendants' motions for judgment on the pleadings.

A. Plaintiffs' Motion for Leave to Amend the Complaint

Having previously amended the complaint, and having previously been denied leave to amend the complaint a second time, plaintiffs once again move for leave to amend the complaint. Plaintiffs seek to add five additional Tennessee state-law claims against defendants and to add Blue Tarp Financial as a defendant, an entity which was previously dismissed from this case. Aside from the situations described in Federal Rule of Civil Procedure 15(a)(1), which do not apply here, "a party may amend its pleading only with the opposing party's written consent or the court's leave." Fed. R. Civ. P. 15(a)(2). "The court should freely give leave," however, "when justice so requires." *Id.* Leave is appropriate "[i]n the absence of . . . undue delay, bad faith or dilatory motive on the part of the movant, repeated failure to cure deficiencies by amendments previously allowed, undue prejudice to the opposing party by virtue of allowance of the amendment, [or] futility of the amendment." *Leary v. Daeschner*, 349 F.3d 888, 905 (6th Cir. 2003) (quoting *Foman v. Davis*, 371 U.S. 178, 182 (1962)); *accord Courie v. Alcoa Wheel & Forged Prods.*, 577 F.3d 625, 633 (6th Cir. 2009). "Amendment of a complaint is futile when the proposed amendment would not permit the complaint to survive a motion to dismiss." *Miller v. Calhoun Cty.*, 408 F.3d 803, 807 (6th Cir. 2005) (citing *Neighborhood Dev. Corp. v. Advisory Council on Historic Pres.*, 632 F.2d 21, 23 (6th Cir. 1980)). The Court will deny plaintiffs' motion for leave to amend on grounds of futility, undue prejudice to defendants, and unnecessary delay. As an initial matter, plaintiffs ask the Court to add Blue Tarp Financial as a defendant pursuant to their proposed second amended complaint. The Court previously dismissed plaintiffs' FDCPA claims against Blue Tarp Financial, finding that Blue Tarp Financial did not attempt to collect a debt from plaintiffs [Doc. 28 p. 20]. That decision remains sound, as the proposed second amended complaint does not allege that Blue Tarp Financial attempted to collect a debt from plaintiffs [Doc. 35-3]. In fact, while plaintiffs request the addition of Blue Tarp Financial in their motion, the proposed second amended complaint does not list Blue Tarp Financial as a defendant in the caption, nor does it list Blue Tarp Financial in the section labeled "parties" where the other defendants are identified [*See id.* at 1–2]. As discussed further below, plaintiffs' FDCPA claims are barred by the applicable statute of limitations because activity associated with the ongoing litigation between the parties is not subject to the continuing violation doctrine and does not constitute a discrete violation of the FDCPA. *Slorp v. Lerner, Sampson, & Rothfuss*, 587 F. App'x 249, 258–59 (6th Cir. 2014). This renders amendment of the complaint futile, as plaintiffs' FDCPA claims will be dismissed, and the remaining claims in the proposed second amended complaint are state-law claims between non-diverse parties over which the Court would decline jurisdiction [*See* Doc. 35-3]; *see also Bowers v. Ophthalmology Gr. LLP*, 648 F. App'x 573, 582 (6th Cir. 2016) ("When all federal claims are dismissed before trial, the balance of considerations usually will point to dismissing the state law claims, or remanding them to state court if the action was removed."). Furthermore, the Court finds that granting leave to amend the complaint would unduly prejudice the defendants and cause unnecessary delay. This is the second time plaintiffs have sought leave to amend the complaint after defendants filed meritorious dispositive motions. While the Court need not decide whether this practice is intended to delay the proceedings, the Court is troubled by this practice, especially considered alongside plaintiffs' other actions, such as their multiple attempts to erroneously remove the underlying state court proceeding to federal court [Case Nos. 3:15-cv-324; 3:17-cv-288]. Defendants have diligently defended this action, and would be prejudiced by the additional delay and expenditure of resources that would be required if the Court were to allow plaintiffs to amend the complaint a second time, as defendants would need to file new dispositive motions or answers in response to the amended complaint.

B. Defendants' Motions for Judgment on the Pleadings

Defendants have moved for judgment on the pleadings with regard to plaintiffs' FDCPA claims.

Defendants argue (1) the FDCPA applies only to family, personal, and household debts, and the alleged debt in the present case is a commercial debt; and (2) plaintiffs' FDCPA claims are barred by the applicable statute of limitations, as activity associated with the ongoing litigation between the parties is not subject to the continuing violation doctrine and does not constitute a discrete violation of the FDCPA. Federal Rule of Civil Procedure 12(c) provides, "After the pleadings are closed— but early enough not to delay trial—a party may move for judgment on the pleadings." The standard of review applicable to a motion for judgment on the pleadings under Rule 12(c) is the same as that for a motion to dismiss under Rule 12(b)(6), and the Court likewise may not consider matters outside the pleadings. *Ziegler v. IBP Hog Mkt., Inc.*, 249 F.3d 509, 511–12 (6th Cir. 2001); Fed. R. Civ. P. 12(d). "All well pleaded material allegations of the non-moving party's pleadings are taken as true and allegations of the moving party that have been denied are taken as false." *Bell v. JP Morgan Chase Bank*, No. 06-

11550, 2006 WL 1795096, at *1 (E.D. Mich. June 28, 2006) (citing *S. Ohio Bank v. Merryl Lynch Pierce Finner and Smith, Inc.*, 479 F.2d 478, 480 (6th Cir. 1973)). The motion should be granted "when no material issue of fact exists and the party making the motion is entitled to judgment as a matter of law." *United States v. Moriarty*, 8 F.3d 329, 332 (6th Cir. 1993) (citation omitted). The Court need not address defendants' first argument, as their second argument, regarding the statute of limitations, is dispositive. A one year statute of limitations applies to FDCPA claims. 15 U.S.C. § 1692k(d). The underlying state-court collection action was filed on November 21, 2012 [Case No. 3:15-cv-324, Doc. 1-2], and the present action was filed on February 16, 2016 [Doc. 1]. Plaintiffs argue two alleged FDCPA violations occurred within the one year limitations period—a hearing before the special master in the underlying state proceeding on February 13, 2015 [Doc. 35-3 p. 16], and a letter from defendants' attorney proposing a settlement conference dated May 28, 2015 [Doc. 1-1 pp. 32–33]—and that the continuing violation doctrine allows for these events to bring previously alleged FDCPA violations, such as the initiation of the underlying collection lawsuit, within the limitations period. This argument is misplaced, as the Sixth Circuit has foreclosed this theory. *Slorp v. Lerner, Sampson, & Rothfuss*, 587 F. App'x 249, 258–59 (6th Cir. 2014). In *Slorp*, the plaintiff brought an FDCPA claim in relation to an allegedly deceptive state-court proceeding. The district court found that the plaintiff's FDCPA claim was barred by the statute of limitations. On appeal, the plaintiff argued (1) his FDCPA claim was not barred by the statute of limitations due to the application of the continuing violation doctrine; and (2) submitting an affidavit to the court pursuant to the state court litigation constituted an independent, unprecluded violation of the FDCPA. *Id.* at 257. The Sixth Circuit found that "application of the continuing violation doctrine to FDCPA claims would be inconsistent with the principles underlying the Supreme Court's limited endorsement of that doctrine in [*National Railroad Passenger Corp. v.*

Morgan, 536 U.S. 101 (2002)]." *Id.* at 258. According to the court, an FDCPA claim based on an allegedly unfair lawsuit accrues on the date the suit is filed, and "initiation of the suit [is] a discrete, immediately actionable event." *Id.* Additionally, the Court found: A plaintiff who alleges several FDCPA violations, some of which occurred within the limitations period and some of which occurred outside that window, will be barred from seeking relief for the untimely violations, but that plaintiff may continue to seek relief for those violations that occurred within the limitations period. But the violations that occur within the limitations window must be discrete violations; they cannot be the later effects of an earlier time-barred violation . . . . The defendants' deceptive conduct, as alleged in the complaint, consisted of their initiation of unfair, misleading, and abusive legal process against Slorp and their concurrent docketing of a fraudulent assignment. The defendants did not commit a fresh violation of the FDCPA each time they filed pleadings or memoranda reaffirming the legitimacy of their state-court suit; rather, those were the continuing effects of their initial violation. *Id.* at 259 (internal citations omitted). Here, plaintiffs attempt to make the same arguments rejected by the Sixth Circuit in *Slorp*. First, plaintiffs may not rely on the continuing violation doctrine to bring FDCPA claims based on events which occurred beyond the limitations period. Second, the discrete events plaintiffs allege took place within the limitations period—the hearing before the special master and the letter requesting a settlement conference—are continuing effects of the underlying state-court lawsuit, which was filed beyond the limitations period, and are thus not themselves discrete violations of the FDCPA which occurred within the limitations period. Plaintiffs thus allege no discrete violations of the FDCPA within the limitations period, and therefore their FDCPA claims must be dismissed pursuant to 15 U.S.C. § 1962k(d).

CONCLUSION

For the reasons stated above, plaintiffs' motion for leave to amend the complaint [Docs. 35, 36] will be DENIED, and defendants' motions for judgment on the pleadings [Docs. 32, 33, 48] will be GRANTED. ORDER ACCORDINGLY.

s/ Thomas A. Varlan, CHIEF UNITED STATES DISTRICT JUDGE

Order for Dismissal

Case No. 3:16-cv-0078, DOC 28 , filed March 28, 2017

UNITED STATES DISTRICT COURT - EASTERN DISTRICT OF TENNESSEE

William Kinney and Margaret Kinney,

v. ANDERSON LUMBER COMPANY, INC., BLUE TARP FINANCIAL, INC., KIZER & BLACK ATTORNEYS, PLLC., McDONALD, LEVY, & TAYLOR, P.C., and JASON ROSE.

MEMORANDUM OPINION AND ORDER

This civil action is before the Court on the following motions: (1) Anderson Lumber Company, Inc.'s Motion to Dismiss [Doc. 4]; (2) McDonald, Levy & Taylor, P.C.'s Motion to Dismiss and/or Motion for Judgment on the Pleadings [Doc. 5]; (3) Kizer & Black, Attorneys, PLLC's Motion to Dismiss Pursuant to Federal Rule of Civil Procedure 12(b)(6) [Doc. 6]; (4) Jason Rose's Motion to Dismiss Pursuant to Federal Rule of Civil Procedure 12(b)(6) [Doc. 7]; (5) Blue Tarp Financial, Inc.'s Motion to Dismiss [Doc. 14]; (6) plaintiffs' Motion to Amend Original Complaint [Doc. 23]; (7) plaintiffs' Motion for Leave to File Supplemental Brief to Defendant's Several Motions to Dismiss [Doc. 24]; and (8) defendants' Motion to Extend Stay [Doc. 25].[1] The parties filed several responses and replies in support of, and in opposition to, the motions before the Court [Docs. 9–12, 15]. For the reasons that follow, the Court will: (1) grant in part and deny in part

---

[1] Also pending is plaintiffs' Motion to Enjoin State Court Proceedings [Doc. 26]. As this motion is not yet ripe for consideration, the Court will defer ruling on it.

Anderson Lumber Company, Inc.'s Motion to Dismiss [Doc. 4]; (2) grant in part and deny in part McDonald, Levy & Taylor, P.C.'s Motion to Dismiss and/or Motion for Judgment on the Pleadings [Doc. 5]; (3) grant in part and deny in part Kizer & Black, Attorneys, PLLC's Motion to Dismiss Pursuant to Federal Rule of Civil Procedure 12(b)(6) [Doc. 6]; (4) grant Jason Rose's Motion to Dismiss Pursuant to Federal Rule of Civil Procedure 12(b)(6) [Doc. 7]; (5) grant Blue Tarp Financial, Inc.'s Motion to Dismiss [Doc. 14]; (6) deny plaintiffs' Motion to Amend Original Complaint [Doc. 23]; (7) grant plaintiffs' Motion for Leave to File Supplemental Brief to Defendant's Several Motions to Dismiss [Doc. 24]; and (8) deny as moot defendants' Motion to Extend Stay [Doc. 25].

I. **Procedural History**[2]

---

[2] The Sixth Circuit has provided that in deciding motions to dismiss pursuant to Rule 12(b)(6), courts may consider "the Complaint and any exhibits attached thereto, public records, items appearing in the record of the case and exhibits attached to defendant's motion to dismiss so long as they are referred to in the Complaint and are central to the claims

On March 21, 2016, the Court entered an Order declaring that the instant matter is related to *Anderson Lumber Co. v. Kinney*, No. 3:15-CV-324 [Doc. 2].[11] In the previously-filed, related action, the parties filed numerous exhibits detailing the procedural history of the case. This matter originated when defendant Anderson Lumber Company, Inc. ("Anderson") filed a complainton November 21, 2012, against "Chris Kinney and Margaret Kinney, d/b/a Kinney Custom Interiors," in the Circuit Court for Blount County, Tennessee, Equity Division ("the state action") [3:15-CV-324,

---

contained therein." Bassett v. Nat'l Collegiate Athletic Ass'n, 528 F.3d 426, 430 (6th Cir. 2008) (citing Amini v. Oberlin Coll., 259 F.3d 493, 502 (6th Cir. 2001)). Defendants cited to the procedural history in this matter throughout their motions to dismiss, and plaintiffs did not object to the Court's consideration of that history. In addition, the Court finds that the procedural history in this matter is central to plaintiffs' claims.

Doc. 3 pp. 7–8]. In the complaint underlying the state action, Anderson sought recovery of $34,765.98 from the Kinneys for "supplies and materials" allegedly purchased by them from Anderson [*Id.*]. Anderson's corporate attorney, John T. McArthur of the firm Kizer & Black, Attorneys, PLLC ("K&B"), filed the state action [*Id.* at 8]. On August 11, 2014, the state court added William Kinney as an additional defendant to the action [*Id.* at 12].

[3] Unless otherwise indicated, citations to the record refer to the docket sheet in Kinney v. Anderson Lumber Co., No. 3:16-CV-78. On December 2, 2014, the Circuit Court for Blount County issued an order referring the case to a Special Master, Jason Rose [3:15-CV-324, Doc. 1-2 pp. 85–86]. A hearing was held on February 13, 2015, and Special Master Rose issued a report on April 30, 2015 [3:15-CV-323, Doc. 3 pp. 15–19]. He determined that that the Kinneys owed Anderson $32,912.95 [*Id.*]. On July 28, 2015, the Kinneys attempted to remove the state action to federal court by filing a notice of removal [3:15-CV-

324, Doc. 1]. Anderson then filed a motion to remand [3:15-CV-324, Doc. 3], which this Court granted [3:15-CV-324, Docs. 7, 8]. On February 16, 2016, plaintiffs filed the present action [Doc. 1].

II. Allegations in the Instant Complaint

In the present action, plaintiffs assert claims against: (1) Anderson; (2); Anderson's finance company, Blue Tarp Financial, Inc. ("Blue Tarp"); (3) Anderson's corporate attorneys, K&B; (4) Anderson's defense attorneys, McDonald, Levy & Taylor, P.C. ("McDonald"); and (5) Jason Rose, the Special Master. Plaintiffs allege claims against defendants pursuant to: (1) the Fair Debt Collection Practices Act ("FDCPA"), 15 U.S.C. § 1692 *et seq.*; (2) the Electronic Funds Transfer Act ("EFTA"), 15 U.S.C. § 1693 *et seq.*; (3) 42 U.S.C. §§ 1983, 1985 for violations of plaintiffs' First, Fourth, and Fourteenth Amendment rights; and (4) 15 U.S.C. § 6821 (Privacy Protection for Customer Information of Financial Institutions). The Court will detail plaintiffs' allegations in support of plaintiffs' claims under each statute in turn.

A. FDCPA Claims

Plaintiffs assert that Anderson initiated the state action based on Anderson's Vice President, Landon Coleman's, sworn account that Margaret and William Kinney financed material through Anderson and owed Anderson money [Doc. 1 ¶ 18]. They further allege that there was no such agreement between William or Margaret Kinney and Anderson [*Id.*]. According to plaintiffs, when plaintiffs' former counsel asked Anderson to produce such documentation, Anderson failed to do so [*Id.*]. As such, plaintiffs assert that "defendants have made false representations regarding a debt allegedly owed by William and Margaret Kinney, by attempting to collect a debt not authorized by any agreement" [*Id.* ¶ 17]. Plaintiffs further allege that the state action constitutes an "unfair and unconscionable means to collect or attempt to collect" debt [*Id.* ¶ 18]. They also contend that they did not enter into a contract with Anderson containing an agreement to pay attorney's fees and that defendants' alleged threats concerning such fees are unlawful [*Id.* ¶ 19].

B. EFTA Claims

Plaintiffs allege that on August 24, 2012, Anderson reopened Margaret Kinney's financial account, which Blue Tarp had previously closed, without her permission and applied five forged invoices to the account [*Id.* ¶ 21; Doc. 1-1 p. 7]. They assert that this action constituted an unauthorized electronic funds transfer [Doc. 1 ¶ 21]. When Margaret Kinney reported the unauthorized transfer to Blue Tarp, plaintiffs assert that Blue Tarp rescinded its payment to Anderson in an effort to deflect its liability under the EFTA [*Id.*]. Anderson then sued Margaret Kinney for the transfer, which, according to plaintiffs, was not only unauthorized, but was also fraudulent [*Id.*].

C. 42 U.S.C. §§ 1983, 1985 Claims

According to plaintiffs, during each of the five judicial hearings held in the state action, beginning on July 1, 2013, and continuing until February 13, 2015, the Honorable David R. Duggan, Judge of the Blount County Circuit Court, along with defendants, deliberately and willfully conspired to deprive plaintiffs of their rights under the First, Fourth, and Fourteenth Amendments of the United States Constitution without due process of law [*Id.* ¶¶ 22–23]. During a hearing on July 1, 2013, the state court did not allow plaintiffs the opportunity to present their motion for summary judgment, motion to compel, motion for a protective order, or motion to intervene [*Id.* ¶¶ 24–27]. At the same hearing, the court granted Anderson's motion to compel the depositions of Chris and Margaret Kinney [*Id.* ¶ 25]. Plaintiffs contend that during the resulting depositions, Anderson coerced plaintiffs into giving private information in the form of sworn testimony and to furnish documents, all without due process [*Id.* ¶ 26]. On August 11, 2014, the state court held another hearing, during which plaintiffs contend that Anderson coerced William Kinney into becoming a defendant in the state action [*Id.* ¶ 28]. Also during this hearing, counsel for Anderson moved the court to appoint a Special Master, and the court granted the motion [*Id.*]. Plaintiffs contend that William Kinney did not have advance notice of this motion or the opportunity to present written or oral objections [*Id.*]. At a hearing on December 1, 2014, William Kinney presented a motion to dismiss, which the state court allegedly declined to address, and he further argued that the order for a Special Master was in violation of his right to due process [*Id.* ¶ 29]. Judge Duggan then appointed Jason Rose as Special Master [*Id.*]. Plaintiffs contend that Judge Duggan's order appointing a Special Master is "void and unenforceable" [*Id.* ¶ 30]. On February 13, 2015, Jason Rose held a hearing in his capacity as Special Master [*Id.*]. Plaintiffs contend that Rose accidentally discovered Anderson's fraudulent manipulation of Margaret Kinney's Blue Tarp account when questioning Anderson's Landon Coleman [*Id.*]. They assert that Rose subsequently ceased his questioning because he was under order from the state court "not to bring up or allow to be discussed any of the criminal allegations made by [plaintiffs]" [*Id.*]. Plaintiffs also contend that defendants violated plaintiffs' right to freedom of religion because the state court would not allow William Kinney to represent his wife, Margaret Kinney [*Id.* ¶ 38]. Plaintiffs assert that they are "one person in the eyes of God, and in law" and that they "must stand together in defense of each other" [*Id.*].

D.   15 U.S.C. § 6821 Claims

During the pretrial discovery phase of the state action, plaintiffs allege that "defendants fraudulently assessed Margaret Kinney's financial and personal information by unlawfully obtaining a copy of a commercial credit application" from Blue Tarp [*Id.* ¶ 15]. According to the complaint, K&B solicited Landon Coleman to have Blue Tarp fax K&B the credit application under false pretenses [*Id.*]. Plaintiffs assert that Anderson attached an un-redacted copy of the application to its original and amended complaint in the state action [*Id.*]. On February 12, 2016, William Kinney obtained a copy of the original complaint, with the credit application attached, from the Clerk of Court for the Blount County Circuit Court [*Id.* ¶ 20]. Plaintiffs contend that Margaret Kinney's personal data is still un-redacted [*Id.*].

III. Standard of Review for Motions to Dismiss

Rule 8(a)(2) of the Federal Rules of Civil Procedure sets forth a liberal pleading standard. *Smith v. City of Salem*, 378 F.3d 566, 576 n.1 (6th Cir. 2004). It requires only "'a short and plain statement of the claim showing that the pleader is entitled to relief,' in order to 'give the defendant fair notice of what the . . . claim is and the grounds upon which it rests.'" *Bell Atl. Corp. v. Twombly*, 550 U.S. 544, 555 (2007) (quoting *Conley v. Gibson*, 355 U.S. 41, 47 (1957)). Detailed factual allegations are not required, but a party's "obligation to provide the 'grounds' of his 'entitle[ment] to relief' requires more than labels and conclusions, and a formulaic recitation of the elements of a cause of action will not do." *Id.* (quoting *Papasan v. Allain*, 478 U.S. 265, 286 (1986)). "Nor does a complaint suffice if it tenders 'naked assertion[s]' devoid of 'further factual enhancement.'" *Ashcroft v. Iqbal*, 556 U.S. 662, 678 (2009) (quoting *Twombly*, 550 U.S. at 557)). In deciding a Rule 12(b)(6) motion to dismiss, the Court must determine whether the complaint contains "enough facts to state a claim to relief that is plausible on its face." *Twombly*, 550 U.S. at 570. In doing so, the Court "construe[s] the complaint in the light most favorable to the plaintiff, accept[s] its allegations as true, and draw[s] all reasonable inferences in favor of the plaintiff." *Directv, Inc. v. Treesh*, 487 F.3d 471, 476 (6th Cir. 2007) (citation omitted). "A claim has facial plausibility when the plaintiff pleads factual content that allows the court to draw the reasonable inference that the defendant is liable for the misconduct alleged." *Iqbal*, 556 U.S. at 678 (citing *Twombly*, 550 U.S. at 556). "Determining whether a complaint states a plausible claim for relief will . . . be a context-specific task that requires the reviewing court to draw on its judicial experience and common sense." *Id.* at 679 (citation omitted). Pro se litigants "are held to less stringent [pleading] standards than . . . lawyers in the sense that a pro se complaint will be liberally construed in determining whether it fails to state a claim upon which relief could be granted." *Jourdan v. Jabe*, 951 F.2d 108, 110 (6th Cir. 1991) (citing *Estelle v. Gamble*, 429 U.S. 97, 106 (1976)). Yet, this Court's "lenient treatment generally accorded to pro se litigants has limits." *Pilgrim v. Littlefield*, 92 F.3d 413, 416 (6th Cir. 1996). "Neither [this] Court nor other courts . . . have been willing to abrogate basic pleading essentials in pro se suits." *Wells v. Brown*, 891 F.2d 591, 594 (6th Cir. 1989). For instance, federal pleading standards do not permit pro se litigants to proceed on pleadings that are not readily comprehensible. *See Becker v. Ohio State Legal Servs. Ass'n*, 19 F. App'x 321, 322 (6th Cir. 2001) (upholding a district court's dismissal of a pro se complaint containing "vague and conclusory allegations unsupported by material facts").

IV. Motion to Amend

Although plaintiffs filed their motion to amend after defendants filed their motions to dismiss, granting a motion to dismiss before addressing a pending motion to amend can be an abuse of discretion. *See Thompson v. Superior Fireplace Co.*, 931 F.2d 372, 374 (6th Cir. 1991). As such, the Court first considers plaintiffs' motion to amend and will then turn to defendants' dispositive motions. Aside from the situations described in Federal Rule of Civil Procedure 15(a)(1), which do not apply here, "a party may amend its pleading only with the opposing party's written consent or the court's leave." Fed. R. Civ. P. 15(a)(2). "The court should freely give leave," however, "when justice so requires." *Id.* Leave is appropriate "[i]n the absence of . . . undue delay, bad faith or dilatory motive on the part of the movant, repeated failure to cure deficiencies by amendments previously allowed, undue prejudice to the opposing party by virtue of allowance of the amendment, [or] futility of the amendment." *Leary v. Daeschner*, 349 F.3d 888, 905 (6th Cir. 2003) (quoting *Foman v. Davis*, 371 U.S. 178, 182 (1962)); *see also Courie v. Alcoa Wheel & Forged Prods.*, 577 F.3d 625, 633 (6th Cir. 2009). "Amendment of a complaint is futile when the proposed amendment would not permit the complaint to survive a motion to dismiss." *Miller v. Calhoun Cty.*, 408 F.3d 803, 807 (6th Cir. 2005) (citing *Neighborhood Dev. Corp. v. Advisory Council on Historic Pres.*, 632 F.2d 21, 23 (6th Cir. 1980)). Furthermore, Local Rule 15.1 pertains to motions to amend and provides the following: A party who moves to amend shall attach a copy of the proposed amended pleading to the motion. Any amendment to a pleading, whether filed as a matter of course or upon a motion to amend, shall, except by leave of the Court, reproduce the entire pleading as amended and may not incorporate any prior pleading by reference. A failure to comply with this rule may be grounds for denial of the motion. E.D. Tenn. L.R. 15.1. The Court first notes that in filing its motion to amend, plaintiffs did not comply with Rule 15.1. Plaintiffs did not attach a copy of their proposed amended complaint to their motion, but instead asserted new allegations within the motion itself [Doc. 23]. In addition, the Court notes that plaintiff did not "reproduce the entire pleading as amended," as required by the Rule 15.1. E.D. Tenn. L.R. 15.1. This is evidenced by the fact that plaintiffs' motion to amend is eight pages [Doc. 23], while their original complaint is twenty-four pages [Doc. 1]. The Court notes that plaintiffs' failure to comply with Rule 15.1 is sufficient justification for the Court to deny plaintiffs' motion to amend. In addition, plaintiffs provide no justification in their motion as to why they delayed in seeking leave to amend. Plaintiffs filed their initial complaint on February 16, 2016 [Doc. 1], and their motion to amend on February 7, 2017 [Doc. 23]. Upon review of the motion to amend, it does not appear that any of the events giving rise to the amendments took place after February 16, 2016 [*See id.*]. To the extent that plaintiffs move to amend their complaint in an attempt to correct the issues raised in defendants' motions to dismiss, the Court notes that plaintiff moved to amend nearly six months after the most recently filed motion to dismiss [*See id.* (motion to amend was filed on February 7, 2016); Doc. 14 (most recent motion to dismiss was filed on August 19, 2016)]. In addition, as discussed herein, the Court finds that plaintiffs' proposed amendments are futile. In their motion to amend, plaintiffs assert that defendants violated the Racketeer Influenced and Corrupt Organizations Act ("RICO"), 18 U.S.C. § 1961 *et seq.*, the Hobbs Act, 18 U.S.C. § 1951, and the Fair Credit Reporting Act ("FCRA"), 15 U.S.C. § 1681 *et seq.* The Court will address the futility of these clams in turn.

A. RICO Claim

To state a RICO claim, a plaintiff must plead four elements: "(1) conduct (2) of an enterprise (3) through a pattern (4) of racketeering activity." *Moon v. Harrison Piping Supply*, 465 F.3d 719, 723 (6th Cir. 2006). A "pattern of racketeering activity" consists of at least two predicate acts of racketeering activity occurring within a ten-year period. 18 U.S.C. § 1961(5); *see also id.* § 1961(1) (listing predicate acts). The plaintiff must further show a "relationship between the predicates and the threat of continuing activity." *Moon*, 465 F.3d at 724 (quoting *H.J., Inc. v. Nw. Bell Tele. Co.*, 492 U.S. 229, 239 (1989)). "The requirement of 'continuity,' or a threat of continuing criminal activity, ensures that RICO is limited to addressing Congress's primary concern in enacting the statute, i.e. long-term criminal conduct." *Vemco, Inc. v.* 34 (6th Cir. 1994). There are two kinds of continuity: "'closed-ended,' referring to a closed period of repeated conduct extending over a substantial period of time, or 'openended,' referring to past conduct 'which by its very nature projects into the future with a threat of repetition.'" *Id.* (quoting *H.J.*, 492 U.S. at 241–42). A short-term scheme directed at a particular finite goal may be "by its very nature, insufficiently protracted to qualify as a RICO violation." *Thompson v. Paasche*, 950 F.2d 306, 311 (6th Cir.

1991). In their proposed complaint, plaintiffs generally allege that Anderson and Blue Tarp participated in a scheme to extort money from Chris Kinney. Specifically, they allege that Anderson and Blue Tarp engaged in extortion, forgery, misuse of financial information, fraud, and other illegal actions, in order to manipulate two of Chris Kinney's financial accounts. The alleged actions giving rise to the RICO claim occurred between August 2011, and August 2012.[4] Taking plaintiffs allegations as true, it appears that the goal of the alleged scheme was to collect approximately $32,000 allegedly owed by Chris Kinney. Plaintiffs have not specified whether they intend to rely on closed-ended or openended continuity. Upon review of their proposed complaint, however, plaintiffs have not provided any facts suggesting that there is any reason to believe that this alleged scheme might be repeated. As such, plaintiffs have not sufficiently alleged a scheme with openended continuity. *See Vemco*, 23 F.3d at 133–34. As to closed-ended continuity, the Court finds that plaintiffs have not pleaded facts sufficient to prevail on their proposed RICO claim because the alleged scheme is

---

[4] Plaintiffs also allege that Anderson violated the Hobbs Act, a predicate act for a RICO claim, in May of 2015 [Doc. 23 ¶ 3]. *See* 18 U.S.C. § 1961(1) (listing predicate offenses). A plaintiff can establish a violation of the Hobbs Act by showing that a defendant induced or attempted to induce the victim to part with property, including intangible property, by extortion or robbery, and that interstate commerce was delayed, interrupted, or adversely effected. *See* 18 U.S.C. § 1951(a). In the context of the Hobbs Act, "[t]he term 'extortion' means the obtaining of property from another, with his consent, induced by wrongful use of actual or threatened force, violence, or fear, or under color of official right." *Id.* § 1951(b)(2).

Plaintiffs contend that "Anderson sent an extortionate demand letter threatening William Kinney with criminal prosecution under the State's

UPL statutes, if the Kinney's did not meet Anderson's demands and pay the sum of approximately $32,000.00" [Doc. 23 ¶ 3 (citing Doc. 11 pp. 32–33)]. Upon review of the cited letter, which plaintiffs attached to their original complaint, the letter does not reference a criminal prosecution [Doc. 1-1 pp. 32–33]. Rather, the letter is from Anderson's counsel, and he is requesting that plaintiffs engage in settlement negotiations [*Id.*]. Even if threatening criminal prosecution is sufficient to constitute extortion— a finding the Court is not making—it does not appear from this letter that Anderson was threatening such action. As such, the Court finds that the sending of this letter in May of 2015 does not constitute extortion and, therefore, is not a predicate RICO offense. The remaining alleged predicate offenses occurred between August 2011, and August 2012. inherently limited. Plaintiffs have not alleged any facts in their proposed complaint to suggest that once they paid the $32,000 allegedly owed, the scheme would not end. The Sixth Circuit has consistently determined that such finite, limited schemes are not within the ambit of the RICO statute. *See, e.g., Moon*, 465 F.3d 719, 723 (finding that an alleged scheme originating from a dispute about whether the plaintiff was impaired by a workplace disability entitling him to benefits did not give rise to RICO continuity); *Vemco*, 23 F.3d at 134–35 (determining that a single scheme stemming from a dispute over an ordinary construction contract did not possess the requisite RICO continuity); *Paasche*, 950 F.2d at 311 (finding that an alleged scheme involving the fraudulent sale of nineteen parcels of land was finite and insufficient to constitute RICO continuity). As such, the Court finds that plaintiffs' allegations concerning Anderson and Blue Tarp's purported scheme do not establish requisite continuity to sustain a RICO claim, and, therefore, plaintiffs' proposed RICO claim is futile.

B.   Hobbs Act Claim

In their proposed amended complaint, plaintiffs assert that defendants violated the Hobbs Act [Doc.

23 p. 1]. Upon review of the proposed complaint, it is unclear if plaintiffs are alleging that defendants violated the Hobbs Act solely because a violation of the Hobbs Act can serve as a predicate offense for a RICO violation, or if plaintiffs are asserting that defendants' alleged violation of the Hobbs Act serves as an independent claim. To the extent that plaintiffs are alleging an independent claim based on the Hobbs Act, the Court notes that the Hobbs Act is a criminal statute and does not provide a private right of action. *See Hopson v. Shakes*, No. 3:12-CV-722-M, 2013 WL 1703862, at *2 (W.D. Ky. Apr. 19, 2013) ("[F]ederal courts have consistently found that the Hobbs Act does not support a private cause of action."). As such, any independent claim based on the Hobbs Act would not survive a motion to dismiss and is futile. If plaintiffs included the Hobbs Act allegations in support of their RICO claim, the Court notes that it has already determined that plaintiffs' RICO claim would not withstand a motion to dismiss because plaintiffs have not alleged sufficient facts to support RICO

continuity. As such, the Court finds that plaintiffs' proposed claim pursuant to the Hobbs Act would not survive a motion to dismiss and is futile.

C. FCRA Claims

Plaintiffs also seek to amend their complaint to add claims pursuant to the FCRA [Doc. 23 p. 1]. The FCRA regulates the activities of "consumer reporting agencies" in order to protect consumers. 15 U.S.C. § 1681(b). Plaintiffs contend that "when Blue Tarp provided Anderson and their counsel with the same information a credit reporting agency would report only to another lender or credit bureau, they served the function of a credit reporting agency, and violated 15 U.S.C. § 1681" [Doc. 23 ¶ 6]. In their proposed amended complaint, however, plaintiffs do not cite any specific provisions of the FCRA that they allege defendants violated. Rather than citing to specific provisions in their proposed amended complaint, plaintiffs reference their response to Blue Tarp's motion to dismiss, in which they assert that Blue Tarp violated 15 U.S.C. §§ 1681a, 1681b, 1681r, and 1681q, and that Blue Tarp is subject to civil liability under §§ 1681n and 1681o for such violations [Doc. 15 pp. 5–9]. As plaintiffs do not repeat these allegations in their proposed complaint, the Court need not consider them in determining whether plaintiffs have stated valid claims under the FCRA. Upon review of the allegations in the proposed amended complaint, the Court finds that plaintiffs' allegations consist of conclusory assertions that defendants violated the FCRA. The complaint does not specify which provisions of the FCRA were violated and how they were violated. Such conclusory assertions are not sufficient to survive a motion to dismiss. *See Twombly*, 550 U.S. at 555. In addition, even if the Court considers the additional allegations contained in plaintiffs' response to Blue Tarp's motion to dismiss, the Court finds that plaintiffs' proposed FCRA claims still would not survive a motion to dismiss. In their response to Blue Tarp's motion to dismiss, plaintiffs contend that defendants violated "15 U.S.C. § 1681a(3), by committing [i]dentity theft in the furtherance of a fraud against the Kinney's [sic]" [Doc. 15 p. 8]. While plaintiffs cited to § 1681a(3), that provision does not exist. It appears that plaintiffs intended to cite § 1681a(q)(3), which provides: "The term 'identity theft' means a fraud committed using the identifying information of another person, subject to such further definition as the Bureau may prescribe, by regulation." 15 U.S.C. § 1681a(q)(3). Section 1681a(q)(3) provides only a definition for "identity theft" as used in the subchapter and does not contain any prohibition or requirement that that Blue Tarp could have violated. As such, any claims pursuant to § 1681a(q)(3) would not survive a motion to dismiss. Plaintiffs also assert that Blue Tarp violated § 1681b. Section 1681b(a) sets out a series of circumstances under which a consumer reporting agency may furnish a consumer report. *Id.* § 1681b(a). The section further provides that a consumer reporting agency may not furnish a consumer report under any circumstance other than those specifically described in the statute. *Id.* Upon review of plaintiffs' proposed amended complaint, plaintiffs' initial complaint, and even considering the allegations set forth in plaintiffs' response to Blue Tarp's motion to dismiss, the Court finds that plaintiffs have not pled sufficient facts upon which the Court can determine whether Blue Tarp furnished a consumer report under the circumstances set forth in § 1681b(a). While plaintiffs allege that Blue Tarp violated § 1681b, they do so in a conclusory manner, in that they not provide sufficient facts establishing the circumstances upon which the disclosure occurred. Without alleging facts to support such conclusions, the Court finds that plaintiffs' alleged claim based on Blue Tarp's violation of § 1681b(a) would not survive a motion to dismiss. *See Twombly*, 550 U.S. at 555. Plaintiffs further allege that Blue Tarp violated § 1681r, which provides: "Any officer or employee of a consumer reporting agency who knowingly and willfully provides information concerning an individual from the agency's files to a person not authorized to receive that information shall be fined under Title 18, imprisoned for not more than 2 years, or both." 15 U.S.C. § 1681r. Plaintiffs contend that Blue Tarp violated this provision by disclosing Margaret Kinney's credit data [Doc. 15 p. 8]. Although § 1681r is a criminal statute, the Sixth Circuit has held that a consumer injured by a violation thereof may sue under § 1681n, which provides a private right of action for willful failure to comply with "any requirement" of the FCRA. *See Kennedy v. Border City Savings & Loan Ass'n*, 747 F.2d 367, 369 (6th Cir. 1984). As the Court has already discussed, however, plaintiffs have not pleaded sufficient facts to establish whether Blue Tarp disclosed any consumer information unlawfully. Consequently, plaintiffs' alleged claim pursuant to § 1681r would not survive a motion to dismiss and is, therefore, futile. Lastly, plaintiffs contend that Blue Tarp violated § 1681q, which provides: "Any person who knowingly and willfully obtains information on a consumer from a consumer reporting agency under false pretenses shall be fined under Title 18, imprisoned for not more than 2 years, or both." 15 U.S.C. § 1681q. Plaintiffs, however, provide no factual allegations to support the conclusion that Blue Tarp obtained plaintiffs' information under false pretenses. As such, the Court finds that plaintiffs' proposed claim based on § 1681q would not survive a motion to dismiss. In sum, the Court finds that none of plaintiffs' proposed amendments would survive a motion to dismiss and, consequently, that those amendments are futile. As such, the Court will deny plaintiffs' motion to amend.

V. Motion to File Supplemental Brief

Plaintiffs request leave to file a supplemental brief in opposition to defendants' motions to dismiss. Defendants did not file a response opposing this request. The Court will grant plaintiffs' motion and will consider this supplemental brief [Doc. 24] in coming to its conclusion.

VI. Motions to Dismiss

The Court now turns to defendants' motions to dismiss, in which defendants move the Court to dismiss all claims in plaintiffs' complaint [Docs. 4–7, 14]. As an initial matter, the Court notes that plaintiffs include additional allegations in their responses to defendants' motions to dismiss that are not contained in their complaint [*See generally* Docs. 9–12, 15]. Although courts generally provide pro se plaintiffs with leniency, as evidenced by plaintiffs' pending motion to amend, plaintiffs in this case are aware that they must move to amend their complaint to add additional allegations. As plaintiffs did not move to amend their complaint to add these additional allegations, the Court will not consider them in determining whether plaintiffs have stated valid claims. In considering defendants' motions to dismiss, the Court will address the following claims in turn: (1) FDCPA claims; (2) EFTA claims; (3) claims under 18 U.S.C. § 1983; (4) claims under 18 U.S.C. § 1985; and (5) claims under 15 U.S.C. § 6821.

A. **FDCPA Claims** Plaintiffs assert various claims under the FDCPA [Doc. 1 ¶¶ 2, 17–19]. Plaintiffs allege that defendants violated the FDCPA through their actions and statements in connection with their attempts to collect a debt in the state action. While plaintiffs generally allege that "defendants" violated the FDCPA, the Court finds that plaintiffs' FDCPA allegations pertain only to defendants Anderson , K&B, and McDonald. Plaintiff has not alleged that defendants Blue Tarp or Jason Rose made any statements or performed any actions in an attempt to collect a debt from plaintiffs. The FDCPA's purpose is to protect consumers from debt-collection practices that are misleading and abusive. *Bridge v. Ocwen Fed. Bank, FSB*, 681 F.3d 355, 356 (6th Cir. 2012). It prohibits a debt collector from using "any false, deceptive, or misleading representation or means in connection with the collection of any debt." 15 U.S.C. § 1692e. The FDCPA further provides that "[a] debt collector may not use unfair or unconscionable means to collect or attempt to collect any debt." *Id.* § 1692f. Plaintiffs assert that defendants Anderson, K&B, and McDonald violated the FDCPA by filing and continuing to pursue a fraudulent state court action in an attempt to force plaintiffs to pay a debt that they do not owe. Defendants assert that the Court should dismiss plaintiffs' FDCPA claims because all of plaintiffs' alleged claims are untimely under the applicable statute of limitations. Section 1692k(d) of the FDCPA states that actions arising under the statute must be brought "within one year from the date on which the violation occurs." 15 U.S.C. § 1692k(d). Because Anderson filed the state action on November 21, 2012, and plaintiffs did not file the instant complaint until February 16, 2016, defendants contend that plaintiffs' FDCPA claims are time barred. Defendants do not address, however, plaintiffs' assertions that defendants have continued to violate the FDCPA by making false representations as to the status of the debt throughout the pendency of the state action. Plaintiffs assert that such actions continued through the Special Master hearing on February 13, 2015, and McDonald's May 28, 2015, letter. Defendants provide no argument for why these later alleged actions do not constitute FDCPA violations, and the Court will not *sua sponte* raise issues that defendants themselves have not raised. As such, the Court finds that plaintiffs have alleged that defendants Anderson, K&B, and McDonald committed FDCPA violations within the limitations period. In addition to the statute of limitations argument, K&B and McDonald assert that the Court should dismiss plaintiffs' FDCPA claims against them because the litigation privilege precludes such claims. They contend that their statements made during the course of a judicial proceeding are absolutely privileged. The Supreme Court has held, however, that the FDCPA "does apply to lawyers engaged in litigation," so long as they fall under the other provisions of the FDCPA. *Heintz v. Jenkins*, 514 U.S. 291, 294 (1995). K&B and McDonald have not asserted that they do not otherwise fall under the FDCPA, and they have provided no argument for why the litigation privilege applies to them in the specific context of the FDCPA. As such, defendants' blanket assertion that they are protected by the litigation privilege is not availing. Aside from the statute of limitations and litigation privilege arguments, Anderson, K&B, and McDonald provide no further basis at this stage of the proceedings for the Court to dismiss plaintiffs' FDCPA claims. The Court will not *sua sponte* analyze the elements of plaintiffs' alleged FDCPA claims to determine whether plaintiffs have stated valid claims. The Court will, therefore, deny Anderson, K&B, and McDonald's motions to dismiss as to the FDCPA claims that plaintiffs assert against them.

B.   EFTA Claims

Plaintiffs also claim that Blue Tarp made an unauthorized electronic funds transfer in violation of the EFTA [Doc. 1 ¶ 21]. Pursuant to § 1693m(g), a plaintiff must bring an action under the EFTA "within one year from the date of the occurrence of the violation." 15 U.S.C. § 1693m(g). Plaintiff contends that Blue Tarp's alleged unauthorized electronic funds transfer occurred on August 24, 2012 [Doc. 1 ¶ 21; Doc. 1-1 p. 7]. Because plaintiffs filed this action on February 16, 2016, over one year after the alleged violation of the EFTA, plaintiffs' claim pursuant to the EFTA is time barred. Plaintiffs allege that any applicable statute of limitations should be tolled under the continuing violation doctrine and because defendants engaged in fraudulent concealment. Plaintiffs, however, only assert that they "did not know, until immediately following the special masters meeting on February 13, 2015[,] the method in which a Blue Tarp invoice is created from an Anderson Lumber invoice" [Doc. 1 ¶ 42]. They do not provide any facts to support that defendants fraudulently concealed the transfer. In addition, plaintiffs provide no facts to support that there was any continuing violation of the EFTA. Consequently, because the alleged violation of the EFTA occurred more than one year before plaintiffs filed their complaint, and because plaintiffs' assertion that the statute of limitations should be tolled is without merit, the Court finds that plaintiffs' EFTA claims should be dismissed.

C. Section 1983 Claims

Plaintiffs also assert claims against defendants pursuant to 42 U.S.C. § 1983 [Doc. 1 ¶ 4]. In order to prevail on a § 1983 claim, plaintiffs are required to prove two elements: (1) they were "deprived of a right secured by the Constitution or laws of the United States," and (2) they were "subjected or caused to be subjected to this deprivation by a person acting under color of state law." *Gregory v. Shelby Cty.*, 220 F.3d 433, 441 (6th Cir. 2000). Here, plaintiffs allege that "at each of the five Judicial hearings held in [the state] case, beginning on July 1, 2013, and continuing until the Special Master's hearing on February 13, 2015," defendants and the Honorable David R. Duggan, Judge of the County Circuit Court, "deliberately and willfully conspired to deprive the Plaintiff of" liberty and property rights guaranteed under the First, Fourth, and Fourteenth amendments [Doc. 1 ¶¶ 22–30].

Plaintiffs admit that defendants are not state actors [*See id.* ¶ 23 ("The defendants, although private actors, are inexorably linked to the State actions.")]. Plaintiffs, however, contend that defendants qualify as state actors because they allegedly conspired with Judge Duggan. "If a private party has conspired with state officials to violate constitutional rights, then that party qualifies as a state actor and may be held liable pursuant to § 1983." *Cooper v. Parrish*, 203 F.3d 937, 952 n.2 (6th Cir. 2000). The Supreme Court has held that that "[p]rivate parties who corruptly conspire with a judge in connection with such conduct are thus acting under color of state law within the meaning of § 1983." *Dennis v. Sparks*, 449 U.S. 24, 29 (1980). But "merely resorting to the courts and being on the winning side of a lawsuit does not make a party a co-conspirator or a joint actor with the judge." *Id.* at 28. Rather, to plead a § 1983 conspiracy, plaintiffs must allege that: "(1) a single plan existed, (2) the conspirators shared a conspiratorial objective to deprive the plaintiffs of their constitutional rights, and (3) an overt act was committed." *Revis v. Meldrum*, 489 F.3d 273, 290 (6th Cir. 2007). Upon review of plaintiffs' allegations in their complaint, the Court finds that plaintiffs have not sufficiently alleged the existence of a conspiracy. Plaintiffs do not provide any factual allegations to support that defendants and Judge Duggan jointly agreed to deprive plaintiffs of any federally protected rights. *See Cramer v. City of Detroit*, 267 F. App'x 425, 427 (6th Cir. 2008) (finding that the plaintiff could not sustain a § 1983 conspiracy claim where there was no evidence of "joint activity" between nonstate actors and state actors). Instead, plaintiffs merely conclude that a conspiracy existed. This unsupported conclusion is not sufficient for the Court to find that plaintiffs have stated a valid § 1983 conspiracy claim. *See Twombly*, 550 U.S. at 555. While plaintiffs generally provide that "defendants" are not state actors, they also argue that defendant Jason Rose was acting as a state actor in his capacity as Special Master. Rose argues that he is entitled to immunity for any actions he performed as Special Master. "It is well established that judges are entitled to absolute judicial immunity from suits for money damages for all actions taken in the judge's judicial capacity, unless these actions are taken in the complete absence of any jurisdiction." *Bush v. Rauch*, 38 F.3d 842, 847 (6th Cir. 1994). Absolute judicial immunity has been extended to non-judicial officers who perform "quasi-judicial" duties. *Id.* Quasi-judicial immunity extends to those persons performing tasks so integral or intertwined with the judicial process that these persons are considered an arm of the judicial officer who is immune. *Id.* (citing *Scruggs v. Moellering*, 870 F.2d 376 (7th Cir. 1989)). The Court finds that even if Jason Rose qualifies as a state actor, he is protected by quasi-judicial immunity. Rose was acting pursuant to Judge Duggan's order and was assisting in the ultimate determination of the state action. The Court finds that while acting as Special Master, Rose was "performing tasks so integral or intertwined with the judicial process" that he is protected by immunity. *See id.* Consequently, plaintiffs' § 1983 claim against Rose will be dismissed. In sum, the Court finds that plaintiffs have not pleaded facts sufficient to support finding that defendants are state actors and also have not stated a valid § 1983 conspiracy claim. To the extent that Jason Rose was a state actor, the Court finds that he is entitled to judicial immunity. As such, plaintiffs have not stated valid § 1983 claims against any defendant. The Court will, therefore, dismiss all § 1983 claims contained in the complaint.

D. Section 1985 Claims

Plaintiffs also assert claims pursuant to 42 U.S.C. § 1985 [Doc. 1 ¶ 5]. Specifically, plaintiffs allege that defendants conspired to interfere with plaintiffs' civil rights in violation of 42 U.S.C. § 1985(2) [*Id.* ¶ 34]. Section 1985(2) prohibits "two or more persons [from] conspir[ing]" to interfere with state judicial proceedings "with intent to deny to any citizen the equal protection of the laws." *Alexander v. Rosen*, 804 F.3d 1203, 1207 (6th Cir. 2015). To prevail on a § 1985(2) claim, a plaintiff must allege "some racial, or perhaps class-based invidiously discriminatory animus behind the conspirators' action." *Id.* at 1207–08 (quoting *Griffin v. Breckenridge*, 403 U.S. 88, 102 (1971)). Similar to the Court's analysis under § 1983, the Court finds that plaintiffs have not sufficiently alleged the existence of a conspiracy to deny plaintiffs of their right to equal protection under the law. Plaintiffs' complaint contains only conclusory assertions of a conspiracy, and it does not contain sufficient factual allegations to support those conclusions. Furthermore, plaintiffs do not offer any factual allegations to suggest that defendants were motivated by invidious discrimination. As such, the Court finds that plaintiffs' complaint fails to state a will dismiss all such claims contained in the complaint.

E. Claims Under 15 U.S.C. § 6821

Plaintiffs assert that defendants violated 15 U.S.C. § 6821 by "obtaining the credit app [of Margaret Kinney]" [Doc. 1 ¶ 16]. Section 6821 prohibits obtaining and soliciting customer information of a financial institution under false pretenses. 15 U.S.C. § 6821. Compliance with § 6821 "shall be enforced by the Federal Trade Commission." *Id.* § 6822(a). Courts have consistently held that there is no private right of action under § 6821. *See, e.g., Hall v. Phenix Investigations, Inc.*, No. 3:14-CV-0665-D, 2014 WL 5697856, at *9 (N.D. Tex. Nov. 5, 2014); *Colemon v. Marshall & Ilsley Bank*, No. 06-C0852, 2007 WL. 4305604, at *3 (E.D. Wis. Dec. 7, 2007). As plaintiffs may not maintain a private action under § 6821, the Court finds that plaintiffs' claims pursuant to § 6821 are without merit, and the Court will dismiss such claims.

VII. Motion to Extend Stay

On December 20, 2016, the Honorable H. Bruce Guyton, United States Magistrate Judge, granted defendants' Motion to Stay Discovery [Doc. 20] and provided that: "The parties shall hold a discovery planning meeting as required by Fed. R. Civ. P. Rule 26(f) on or after March 31, 2017" [Doc. 21]. Defendants now move the Court to extend that stay of discovery until it rules on the pending motions to dismiss. As the Court now addresses the motions to dismiss, defendants' requested relief is moot. Consequently, the Court will deny the motion to extend stay as such.

VIII. Conclusion

For the reasons discussed herein, the Court hereby: (1) **GRANTS in part and DENIES in part** Anderson's Motion to Dismiss [Doc. 4]; (2) **GRANTS in part and DENIES in part** McDonald's Motion to Dismiss and/or Motion for Judgment on the Pleadings [Doc. 5]; (3) **GRANTS in part and DENIES in part** K&B's Motion to Dismiss Pursuant to Federal Rule of Civil Procedure 12(b)(6) [Doc. 6]; (4) **GRANTS** Jason Rose's Motion to Dismiss Pursuant to Federal Rule of Civil Procedure 12(b)(6) [Doc. 7]; (5) **GRANTS** Blue Tarp's Motion to Dismiss [Doc. 14]; (6) **DENIES** plaintiffs' Motion to Amend Original Complaint [Doc. 23]; (7) **GRANTS** plaintiffs' Motion for Leave to File Supplemental Brief to Defendant's Several Motions to Dismiss [Doc. 24]; and (8) **DENIES as**

moot defendants' Motion to Extend Stay [Doc. 25]. Accordingly, all claims asserted in plaintiffs' complaint, with the exception of plaintiffs' FDCPA claims against Anderson, McDonald, and K&B, are hereby **DISMISSED.** IT IS SO ORDERED. s/ Thomas A. Varlan CHIEF UNITED STATES DISTRICT JUDGE

CONSTITUTIONAL PROVISIONS, in relevant part;

First Amendment To The United States Constitution, *"Congress shall make no law respecting an establishment of religion, or prohibiting the free exercise thereof; or abridging the freedom of speech, or of the press; or the right of people peaceably to assemble, and to petition the government for a redress of grievances."*

Fifth Amendment To The United States Constitution,

"No person shall be ... compelled in any criminal case to be a witness against himself, nor be deprived

of life, liberty, or property, without due process of law; nor shall private property be taken for public use, without just compensation."

Seventh Amendment To The United States Constitution,

"In Suits at common law, where the value in controversy shall exceed twenty dollars, the right of trial by jury shall be preserved,"

Ninth Amendment To The United States Constitution, *"The enumeration in the Constitution, of certain rights, shall not be construed to deny or disparage others retained by the people."*

Tenth Amendment To The United States Constitution,

The powers not delegated to the United States by the Constitution, nor prohibited by it to the States, are reserved to the States respectively, or to the people.

Fourteenth Amendment To The United States Constitution, Section I,

"No state shall ... deprive any person of life, liberty, or property, without due process of law; nor deny to any person within its jurisdiction the equal protection of the laws."

Federal Statutes

28 U.S. Code § 1254 - Cases in the courts of appeals may be reviewed by the Supreme Court by the following methods: (1) By writ of certiorari granted upon the petition of any party to any civil or criminal case, before or after rendition of judgment or decree;

42 U.S. Code § 1983 - Every person who, under color of any statute, ordinance, regulation, custom, or usage, of any State or Territory or the District of Columbia, subjects, or causes to be subjected, any citizen of the United States or other <u>person</u> within the jurisdiction thereof to the deprivation of any rights, privileges, or immunities secured by the Constitution and laws, shall be liable to the party injured in an action at law, suit in equity, or other proper proceeding for redress, except that in any action brought against a judicial officer for an act or omission taken in such officer's judicial capacity, injunctive relief shall not be granted unless a declaratory decree was violated or declaratory relief was unavailable.

15 U.S. Code § 1692 et seq. The Fair Debt Collection Practices Act

www.ingramcontent.com/pod-product-compliance
Lightning Source LLC
Chambersburg PA
CBHW051322220526
45468CB00004B/1457